I have a passion to develop Chı
some leadership principles are
ment is necessary to achieve success in a ministry workplace. Don Cartmell has captured the essence of this uniqueness, and deals directly with the core issues. His insights and wisdom make this invaluable reading for those who interact with other Christians in workplace or ministry.

Dr. John C Maxwell, author of *The Winning Attitude*

It is sad to see how much manipulation and tyranny is carried on under the guise of Christian ministries. Hearts are broken, careers cratered, and families are often scarred for life. It doesn't need to be this way. *It's Because We're Family* is more than an analysis of the problem—it's a clear solution to the pain. Don Cartmell has written a sensitive book that shows us how to practice in the back offices and board meetings the grace we preach about on Sunday.

Dr. Tim Kimmel, author of *Powerful Personalities*

As Don so relevantly outlines in this book, relational success is the key to the growth of any business or ministry where Christian *family* members are involved. Think of what God could accomplish through the Body of Christ, our family, if these principles were applied in the workplace! Every Christian who works in a business or ministry should read (and apply) what Don shares in this book. "If two of you agree on earth about anything that they may ask, it shall be done for them by my Father who is in heaven" (Matthew 18:19). There would be no limit to what God could do.

Larry Burkett, Founder and CEO,
Christian Financial Concepts, Inc.

Don Cartmell's insights into the hopes and hurts of the modern Christian workplace will help many believers past the expectations of a Christian job being an "early heaven." This resource will help Christian workers relate in a way that keeps the Spirit of Christ in their midst and the spirit of darkness outside. Whether you are a part of a church staff or a Christian type business, you will learn much about the relational risks and opportunities for fulfillment inherent in working and living with "the family."

Dr. Jack Hayford, Senior Pastor,
The Church on the Way, Van Nuys, CA

Don Cartmell has provided us with great insight into why Christians often have a tough time just getting along. This is a great book for in depth answers to our Christian family dilemma.

Stephen Arterburn, Host, New Life Clinic radio broadcast

When Christians work together in a ministry or business, loving relationships develop that last a lifetime. Sometimes these same relationships turn bitter and stressful with the same degree of intensity.

Why is this?

It's because we're family!

Donald V. Cartmell

Camarillo, CA 93012

1998
Published by TEM, Inc.
11 Margarita Avenue, Camarillo, CA 93012

Cover design: Lastra & Associates

Printed in the United States of America

Cartmell, Donald V.
It's Because We're Family
ISBN 0-966496-C-8

1. Christian Leadership 2. Self Help 3. Christians in ministry

1 2 3 4 5 6 7 8 9 10 / 05 04 03 02 01 00 99 98

Contents

Acknowledgments

I am grateful for each person with whom I have worked: in the secular workplace, pastoral ministry, and Christian broadcasting. Each has, in some way, made a contribution to this book by giving me the opportunity to gain valuable insights. Part of my career has been in Christian-formatted radio. This satisfies my definition for a Christian workplace in which, although no employees were subjected to a religious test, the majority were involved because of their compatibility to the format. My role in broadcasting enabled me to interact with the leaders and staffs of many ministries, churches, and ministry-related companies and organizations. Each confirmed the unique dynamics that occur when Christians work together in a workplace environment.

Above all else, I appreciate the value of my wife's input into this project. I cannot begin to count the discussions Nikki and I have had on the subject of this book during the past twenty years. Her insightful perspective helped my thoughts solidify, and her encouragement motivated me into action.

Thank you!

Introduction

Christians working together in ministries or Christian businesses should develop relationships that last a lifetime. A common bond called Calvary links us together. In fact, one of the key "marketing plans" God uses to tell the story of His grace and love is Christians relating with each other in love.

Frequently, for reasons we will discuss as we go along, some of these Christian relationships become injured. This is particularly noticeable when Christians work together in church ministry or some other Christian workplace activity. The January 1998 edition of *Ministries Today* magazine featured an article by Joseph Umidi, which says in part,

> Inter-staff conflict has become a common land mine in the church at large, wounding many of our best emerging leaders. Research from hundreds of pastors, denominational leaders, and clergy retreat centers confirms that more staff relationships are maimed and handicapped by unhealthy conflict resolution practices than by anything else in the enemy's arsenal. It is now the No. 1 reason pastors and church leaders leave the ministry. It is also a key contributor to the fact that 100,000 of the 350,000 churches in America will close their doors in the next three years.

Physicians tell us that cancer cells attack even the healthiest people, every day, seeking an opportunity to live, multiply, and destroy what is good. Only a strong immune system can effectively neutralize their destructive efforts.

Similarly, even the healthiest ministries, and individual Christians in ministry, are under daily attack by cancerous type thoughts that seek to give growth to dissention, jealousy, and greed. These destructive activities can be neutralized only by the presence of a healthy immune system. This book provides insights and solutions to help you develop both a personal and corporate immune system, to provide protection against these attacks.

Experiences shared in this book began about forty-five years ago in the province of British Columbia. I have observed, considered, and contemplated, as my career has taken me into both general market and Christian work environments. I discovered that each had its own unique set of challenges. For example, I noticed that, in the general workplace, the air could turn blue when two people differed, but in a few minutes they were back to work and laughter was soon heard.

Christians working together were different. Here, when relational problems developed, voices were seldom raised. Instead of the air turning blue, it became quiet. Body language was evident. In some cases hard feelings could linger for days, even weeks or months, before parties could resolve their difficulties. Coffee breaks were not always one big happy session in which the room was filled with laughter. Instead, I would frequently observe individual cells of people, usually involved in serious conversation. It wasn't unusual to see people looking burdened or sad. Sometimes this was because of the empathy they had for each other, and other times they were simply nursing hurt feelings.

I found it amazing how those in secular workplaces could usually resolve workplace problems much faster than their Christian counterparts could. I thought it should have been the opposite, reasoning that Christians should have the ability to love, forgive, forget, and exhibit tolerance and understanding. Although these elements were present, they often didn't prevail. Why?

And then it occurred to me: It's Because We Are Family!

As I continued to observe life in the Christian workplace with greater interest, I found that, when things were good, they could be very good. When they were bad, they could be equally bad!

For years, within our church community, I was familiar with the salutations of *brother* and *sister.* I perceived these to be little more than an acknowledgment that we were Christians. Several years ago I finally realized that the Christian family is truly family in a literal as well as a spiritual sense, especially in the context of relationships. This understanding laid the foundation for this book.

I became aware that Christians interacting with each other frequently displayed a family-like tendency toward sibling rivalry. Yes, we are family, but as with all families we sometimes project the wrong identity. I recently heard a professional research specialist discuss the results of an extensive study, which revealed that the lifestyle of Christians was only slightly different from that of those who did not profess Christianity. This isn't the way it was intended to be! Certain aspects of Christian priorities are expected to be distinctly different. Rather than giving in to the tendencies for sibling rivalry and jealousy, Christian family life was supposed to mean brothers and sisters interacting with each other in love (John 13:35).

As you proceed through this book with me, I'm sure you will sense my passion in dealing with these important family issues. You see, the older I get, the more I value my Christian faith and the relationships it provides.

Today, in almost any segment of the Christian workplace, there are those who feel used and disillusioned. As James 3:10 proclaims, "My brothers [and sisters], this should not be" (NIV). If Christians relating to each other in love is to be our badge of identity, then brothers and sisters, let's discover how we can make it happen.

The Christian Workplace Is Vast

Never have more Christians interacted with each other in ministry or business than today. In America, millions are engaged within the Christian workplace. For the purpose of this book, references to either workplace or ministry refers to any place where Christians work together on continuing projects, in ministry or Christian-type business, whether as paid staff, professionals, or volunteers.

Some relational challenges exist within the Christian workplace that are entirely unique. The examples I provide not only illustrate this uniqueness but likely will ring a few bells with you as you recall some of your own experiences. The names and some details of the stories have been altered to ensure the privacy of individuals.

I invite you to view your Christian work or ministry relationships literally through the lenses of your own family experiences. If your family life was not particularly filled with happiness, the following pages may provide insights as to why some things happen as they do. You will become more alert to some of the disciplines needed to protect work or ministry relationships. Similarly, if your family experience was filled with love and caring, this book may help you replicate that experience today in your interaction with other Christians.

To the degree that workers understand the challenges of Christian leadership, their ability to develop and maintain healthy relationships increases proportionately. Similarly, to the degree leaders in ministry gain insight into the work environment they create for others, they become more effective at guiding those in their organizations to relational success.

Are you ready to join me as we drop the façade that so often surrounds those in ministry—to deal with some very real issues?

ONE

The Christian Workplace—Uniquely God's

I RECENTLY VISITED WITH SOMEONE WHO SPENT SEVERAL YEARS in pastoral ministry as an associate in one of the nations' "mega-churches". This ministry is known around the world, and the senior pastor's name is recognized in Christian circles everywhere. This particular ministry has guided thousands into a close relationship with Christ. It is a place of healing, where people grow in their understanding of God's love. This person told me: "Don, that ministry has touched literally millions of lives throughout the world. I have great respect for the pastor. The tragedy is the number of wonderful people who have worked as part of that ministry and have been hurt, bruised, and damaged in the process." Unfortunately, similar situations exist within ministries everywhere. Perhaps your life has been torn through some church experience, either as a volunteer or staff member. Maybe you have asked, "Lord, why is there so much misunderstanding within our organization?" If so, you are not alone—others are asking the same question.

Sensitivity exists between Christians that enables them to develop warm, transparent, and happy relationships. Frequently, however, this same sensitivity makes them especially susceptible to discouragement, confusion, jealousy, and frustration. When hurt or discouraged, Christians may be reluctant to confront each other. Instead, for the sake of the ministry, or the need to be perceived as mature Christians, they suppress their feelings. Some situations never do get resolved.

Jesus said that members of His family would be identified by their ability to relate to each other in love (John 13:35). He intended that members of His family be happy and appreciate each other. It's unrealistic to suggest that relational problems will not exist, but if we address these challenges promptly, many of these difficulties can be resolved.

Christians Take Problems Underground

Two years ago we visited my wife's parents in central British Columbia. They have waterfront property on a secluded lake, miles from any major population center. It is a picturesque setting, with their home nestled among a cluster of pine trees, overlooking a lake where the fish leap playfully out of the water.

A few months before our visit, they had cleared some of the larger pine trees from the property to accommodate development plans. As we ambled down toward the lake, it seemed as though we were walking on a giant cushion, the result of years of decaying leaves and branches. Under the surface there was almost a peat-moss condition. A workman offered to gather the debris from recently felled pine trees and burn them. My father-in-law replied, "No, we won't so much as light a match in this area. We'll carry the branches up to a gravel area to do our burning!"

The reason? If a fire ever got started in that type of ground cover, it would go under the surface and could smolder for months. The fire would move to wherever it could find dry, combustible twigs and leaves to ignite.

So it is in the Christian workplace when relationships become injured and people feel manipulated or used. Rather than confront the individual(s) involved, we tend to bury the hurt underground, where it continues to smolder deep inside.

This can go on for months, even years. As with our illustration, the effect can spread in many directions, drawn perhaps to someone else, equally dry and combustible. It seems we can always find at least one person willing to carry the hurt and unrest a bit farther. Once started, these fires are hard to quench.

Christians are much better at hugging than confronting. You may say, "But Jesus admonished us to be peacemakers!" Indeed He did, and one of the most effective peacemaking skills is the art of loving confrontation. We too often wait until relationships are strained and communication is difficult before acknowledging that a problem must be addressed. By that time it is easier to take a "wait and see" attitude and see if time will heal the wounds. So we let things slide. We discover that time alone doesn't usually heal relational problems—it just gives the parties more time to nurse their hurts. Sometimes a cooling-off period is necessary, but at the earliest appropriate moment, the one who cares the most should initiate a loving, friendly confrontation designed to bring about resolve. This process is called loving one another! (See Chapter 10 for some helpful steps for successful confrontation.)

Christians are better at hugging than confronting!

In the Old Testament we have the account of a workplace where Nehemiah assumed the task of leading members of the Jewish family in rebuilding the wall of Jerusalem. Together they worked side by side and rebuilt the wall of the City of God. They should have been the happiest people on the face of the earth. Perhaps they were, but family tensions developed at a pace that exceeded the wall-building project. In Nehemiah's case, the situation smoldered for a time until some of the workers' emotions reached the boiling point. These hurting workers eventually confronted Nehemiah and made him aware of the serious relational problems that existed between these members of God's family. The problem, it turns out, was usury—the practice of lending money at such high interest rates that, at times, those in debt had to resort to selling themselves or their sons and daughters into slavery (Neh. 5). Nehemiah commanded the unscrupulous lenders to stop the practice immediately, and return whatever they had overcharged to their fellow workers. In making this command, Nehemiah solidified an important principle that applies to us today. His instructions clearly emphasized the valuable relationship the Israelites enjoyed with God. In essence he declared that business arrangements between members of God's family should be designed so that unnecessary stress or bondage is not imposed on other family members.

God does not want members of His family to use one another.

The changes introduced by Nehemiah were significant in that they enabled the Jews to continue assessing usury from the Gentiles, but not from their Jewish countrymen. Why? It's simple—they were family! We discover that these hurt and frustrated people had one thing in common: They were all members of God's family. We acknowledge too that those who imposed the usury were also members of God's family. Working together on this project had jeopardized their relationships.

Through this experience the Jewish people learned that, even at the risk of making some poor business decisions, their heritage as members of God's family was to be part of their business disciplines as well.

They were to protect their relationships with each other—and with God!

Nehemiah emphasized that the work they were doing was too

important to allow avoidable inequities to interfere with progress.

This is also God's message for those of us who have accepted responsibilities within our churches, ministry organizations, or Christian-type businesses. Because of who we are as members of God's family, and because of the eternal importance of the work we are doing, all inequities that have an adverse affect upon our relationships should be eliminated.

I doubt that God's priorities have changed over the years, or He wouldn't have placed such great emphasis on teaching us to love one another, especially our brothers and sisters in Christ. In simplest terms, it is clearly evident that God does not want members of His family to use one another.

Millions of Christians today are volunteering their services within their respective churches and organizations. Some serve on church staffs. Others are involved in Christian-type businesses. Regardless of their ministry or career commitment, many feel trapped. They want to serve God but cannot understand the requests and obligations frequently imposed on them by their fellow Christians. They are victims of a type of "usury" that is not usually recognized as such.

Usury Can Take Many Forms

As in Nehemiah's time, usury still refers to unreasonable financial arrangements. But, when we analyze its meaning further, we can reasonably conclude that it can apply equally to any situation where family members:

- ◆ Take advantage of one another;
- ◆ Expect more from one another than what is reasonable; or
- ◆ Place unfair or unrealistic obligations on one another.

One premise of this book is that, in order to develop and protect lasting relationships, we must ensure that usury of this nature does not exist in our places of ministry. A work environment without usury is where lasting relationships develop!

I recall the occasion when I first discovered my ability to impose usury on a fellow Christian. Years ago, I was interviewing a young man for a position as an announcer on a Christian-formatted radio station. This young man was no novice. He had talent. I was going for minimum wage and could see that I was losing. I knew he was worth much more than I was prepared to pay, but I was determined to hire him at minimum wage for the sake of the ministry. Finally, resorting to my most effective negotiation tool, I reached out to him with great sincerity: "I realize I'm only offering minimum wage but, as a Christian, where could you find a better opportunity to minister to literally thousands of people every day than in the opportunity I am offering you? Perhaps you and your wife should pray about this before you say no."

He accepted—and I won. Or did I?

By knowingly placing "ministry guilt" on him, I manipulated him into working for an organization that could and should have paid him much better than it did. I extracted from that young man an employee value that far exceeded the salary he received. I expected far more from him than I paid in return. It was a case of family using family. Nehemiah would have called it usury!

Should that which was purchased on Calvary be used today as a negotiating tool in business? Should the church environment impose expectations on members of God's family beyond what is reasonable?

I think not.

In developing this book, I perceived two options from which I could choose. One, I could create a book filled with scriptural admonitions as to how to develop good relations within the workplace, such as:

> My friends, we ask you to be thoughtful of your leaders who work hard and tell you how to live for the Lord. Show them great respect, try to get along with each other.

> Encourage anyone who feels left out, help all who are weak, and be patient with everyone. Don't be hateful to people, just because they are hateful to you. Rather, be good to each other and to everyone else. (1 Thes. 5:12-17)

The truth is that we already know how God wants us to relate to each other! As ABC radio commentator Paul Harvey says, "We know much better than we do!"

Why is it that a husband can attend his weekly Rotary Club meeting and be a laugh a minute, but when he steps inside his own house with those he loves, he often becomes quiet and preoccupied? Why do children in a family frequently have more fun playing with the children next door than with each other? When members of family visit friends, why is it they will volunteer to do the dishes and help wherever they are needed—but at home do little or nothing? What is it about family that brings out the best and the worst in people?

The Christian ministry or business is predominately family, and these same tendencies can be observed in varying degrees wherever members of God's family relate on a continuing basis. Why?

My second option seemed to be to answer some of these "whys?"

Will you join me as we take an honest look at some of the challenges inherent within the Christian workplace? As we do, I believe we will discover some ways to enjoy success in our work and ministry relationships.

TWO

The Best of the Best—or the Worst of the Worst?

THIS WEEK, MILLIONS IN AMERICA WILL INVEST TIME AND energy working alongside other Christians in a variety of ministry activities. What should be more fulfilling and enjoyable than interacting with other Christians on a continuing basis? Similarly, singing in the church choir, teaching a Sunday school class, or working as part of the church staff would appear to offer great potential for satisfaction! What employment could offer greater fulfillment than working in some form of ministry-related business? Fortunately, for many today, ministry work is wonderfully fulfilling. On the other hand though, we can find others who have invested years helping in various Christian projects, whose observation would be, "In my case, it was one of the most emotionally difficult experiences of my life!"

An exhilarating and loving atmosphere can be found in many Christian workplaces. However, family tensions occasionally develop that can be extremely hurtful and emotionally draining. The high work ethic within the Christian faith makes it feasible for the Christian workplace to be described as the "best of the best." Sadly, the "worst of the worst" can be just as accurate a description. Is it possible that your work or ministry situation could ever become one of the worst experiences of your life? I don't mean for everyone, but perhaps just for you.

This seems rather strange. Here I am suggesting it is possible to develop and protect relationships within the ministry family and, in almost the same breath, asking if you could imagine your present situation ever becoming an emotionally draining experience. The fact is that the Christian workplace is family. Family enterprises have some inherent risks, often because family members enter the workplace with unrealistic expectations.

The Family—Birthplace of Sibling Rivalry

Sibling rivalry begins at home: it's a family thing. So, for a prime example, let's look at what happens to a typical family at Christmas.

In the Jones family we have father and mother, plus their six grown children and grandchildren. Everyone is gathering at Grandma and Grandpa's for the holidays.

Watch with me as they arrive. As with any family, each sibling has taken a different career path, evident to some degree by the cars they drive. Most arrive in older cars. I see a Toyota, a couple of VWs, a Dodge, a brand new pickup truck—and here comes Charlie and his wife in their new Cadillac! Charlie and his wife recently inherited a sizable sum of money. Unfortunately, their relationships with their brothers and sisters changed as a result of their good fortune. The moment they inherited that money, they began to distance themselves from the rest of the family. They had their reasons.

Now it's Christmas! They all visit for a while as mom cooks the Christmas dinner. Instead of a room filled with laughter and hugs, the family breaks down into little cells, talking in subdued tones. Charlie and his wife are finding things quite awkward. They stay fairly much to themselves, probably out of fear that another member of the family will hit them up for a loan. One already has! Tommy's son needs major surgery, and Tommy and his wife don't have the money to cover the operation. They asked Charlie for a loan, but he turned them down. Charlie felt justified in doing so—he could easily spare the money, but didn't want to open the door to requests for loans from other family members. Charlie is aware that everybody in the room knows about the situation, and is mindful that Tommy's son still needs the operation. Charlie does his best to avoid eye contact with Tommy.

Charlie is disappointed that none of his brothers and sisters congratulated them on their good fortune. No one even commented about his new Cadillac. Isn't it ironical that, even within family, it's often easier to "weep with those who weep" than to "rejoice with those who rejoice"? (Rom. 12:15, NKJV)

Mom and Dad Jones have been looking forward to this day for months, in a way that only parents and grandparents understand. When the last son or daughter moves away from home and the parents are alone, life becomes a blend of remembering the good times, developing a new lifestyle, and anticipating visits from their children. Christmas was one of these special times for the Jones family. In fact, last week, as the parents placed each ornament on the Christmas tree, they couldn't help wiping away nostalgic tears as they remembered Christmases when the children were young.

Today all begin to sing carols and to reminisce about past holidays spent together, but only the youngsters seemed willing or able to get into the Christmas mood. Thank God for the grandchildren! They saved the day simply because they are too young to know how material gains or losses can affect family relationships. In the midst of all the tension, the children play together and enjoy themselves. Looking for safe ground, most of the adults focus their attention on the children instead of each other. It is easier that way. Through the fortune of some and misfortune of others, and the interaction that happens within families, that particular family had become the "worst of the worst," a model of tension and jealousy.

In this case we observed the presence of sibling rivalry, and a situation where family members expect more from each other than was reasonable. Mom and Dad had programmed their expectations so high that they set themselves up for disappointment. The introduction of financial good fortune into that family made all their relationships tense and awkward.

All the factors that enable a family to be close make members equally sensitive to those little comments and events that can turn a relationship sour with equal intensity.

Sibling Rivalry in the Christian Family

Recently a Christian man in his forties said to me, "I've had three very bad experiences dealing with Christian organizations. I find it extremely difficult to trust any more." He placed his hand on my arm, looked me squarely in the face and added, "Help me to trust, I want to!" His eyes seemed to plead, "Surely you can help me! You won't let me down too, will you?"

*Within families—
good things happen to some while
adversity visits others.*

The Christian family is truly family, where brothers and sisters interact with each other on a daily basis. Within all families, good things happen to some while adversity visits others. Not being privy to all that our heavenly Father is about in the lives of each of His children, we tend to draw our own conclusions as to why things happen as they do. Within all families, jealousy can become a factor. Only the mature in Christ seem genuinely able to rejoice with sincerity when others close to them succeed.

In the case of my friend, his loss of trust was the result of this very issue. He didn't know what his heavenly Father was doing in the lives of those who had let him down, so he drew his own conclusions as to their motives. Not being God, he had incomplete information. It so happened that the leaders of these organizations similarly erred and misjudged the motives of my friend. Each expected more from the other than could be realistically given. Each was a case of sibling rivalry where they felt "used" by the other. Each was puzzled by the other person's unreasonable behavior.

History documents the love, warmth, and support found within the growing family. There is nothing on earth that can take its place! As families grow up:

- Love deepens;
- An understanding of each other's uniqueness is gained; and
- Appreciation for one another grows.

However, few families manage to avoid at least some periods of sibling rivalry, especially if family and business activities become entwined. Sometimes:

- Love becomes hate;
- Friendships turn into jealousy and resentment; and
- The closeness of what used to be fades and disappears.

I'm convinced that God had many reasons for referring to us as His "family." First, He wants us to understand the intimacy of our relationship with Him. It is important that we understand that we have access to Him in the same way that children can relate to a loving father. Second, He wants us to learn about His ability and willingness to love and care for us. Third, He desires that we understand how to relate to each other. He longs for us to understand the family concept well, so we can enjoy life with Him, and His family.

He desires that we are family-wise in our interaction with other Christians.

God's Family in Bible Times

A wonderful plan of God has brought us to this place in history. My optimism in regard to Christian relationships is based on the fact that where we are today is part of God's plan, and nothing is more important to Him than the welfare of His family.

Let's take a brief look at our family history.

God created the family unit back in the Garden of Eden, knowing that it would be good—and it was. With infinite wisdom He conceived the concept of a caring husband, and a loving, sensitive wife. He told them to be fruitful and multiply.

Together as father and mother, they were to love and care for their children and guide them into adulthood. The family concept had begun, and what a beautiful concept it was!

And Then Sin Entered The Picture

The book of Genesis records the tragic event when the family concept became infected by sin. From that time on, no one has been exempt from the temptation to

- ◆ Control others
- ◆ Achieve success at the expense of others
- ◆ Strive for importance and power
- ◆ Use all of the above methods for material gain.

From that point on, family relationships were at risk!

Since the introduction of sin into the human race, relational success between family members has required an ongoing commitment to certain priorities, disciplines, and safeguards. Even then, there are no guarantees of success.

In the Old Testament, we observed the individual family concept emerge into something larger. Once the idea of the human family was well understood, God enlarged the concept by introducing His very own family! He chose to bless Abraham and his seed and adopted them as family. He loved and cared for the children of Israel in the same way that He desires an earthly father to love and care for his own family. He allowed the children of Israel to discover His ability to lead and provide. He allowed them to grow and mature, to stumble and fall, and then to feel the strength of His strong and protective hand reaching down to them in love to bring healing to their troubled situations, and lead them on.

Where You And I Come In

Through His birth, life, death, and resurrection, Jesus revealed His Father's concept of the family of God, bringing an even deeper understanding and intimacy to that family relationship. He explained to His disciples that He and His Father were One, and that knowing the Son was to know the Father also. He referred to His followers as His brethren (brothers and sisters). He repeatedly encouraged them to love one another. He made frequent references to His Father's house and told His disciples that He would soon be returning to His Father. He also told them that, one day, where He is, they would be also (John 14:1-3). Through the grace of God poured out at Calvary, the scope of His family increased to include all who trust Jesus Christ as Savior and Lord (John 3:16). How we cherish the knowledge that, by faith, we also have become members of His family.

Today, God continues to have great plans for His family. Each member is special to Him. Not only are we to have an intimate relationship with Him, but we are to love and care for each other as well. It is that loving, caring relationship with Him, and with one another, that Jesus said would identify us as being His (John 13:35).

Sibling Rivalry in Bible Times

It is ironic how something as terrific as God's family can have a flip side, but Scripture records many family situations where sibling rivalry was prominently displayed.

The story of Joseph and his family is one example. Here we have a typical middle-class family of Jewish farmers, who tended their flocks. The brothers worked out in the fields, guided by the leadership of their father. This was a family enterprise. However, due to a lack of good judgment on the part of both the father, Jacob, and Joseph, some comments were made and impressions given that inspired hatred and jealousy in the hearts of Joseph's brothers. The result was tragic. His brothers sold Joseph into slavery, and, as if that wasn't enough, they deceived their father by telling him that wild animals had killed Joseph. (It's too bad Jacob couldn't have a DNA test done on the blood stains on Joseph's garment!)

It is that loving, caring relationship with Him, and with one another, that Jesus said would identify us as being His.

Jacob, of course, was broken-hearted, and was caused to mourn the death of his favorite son unnecessarily. What was once an exemplary family became a scene of sorrow, hopelessness, and despair—the worst of the worst.

This was a case of sibling rivalry, coupled with some expectations that exceeded reason. Joseph somehow expected his brothers to receive the proposal that they would eventually kneel to him, a classic example of expecting more from family members than they could reasonably give. We could refer to this as a form of usury. A lack of wisdom evidenced by two members of that family placed all their relationships at risk.

This occurs in today's ministry workplace. What leader has not made it obvious to others that he or she enjoys a special work relationship with a certain individual? What workplace has not experienced repercussions when a favored worker told others prematurely of a planned promotion? Within the dynamics of family, workers are sensitive to these issues.

We can also read the biblical account of Jacob and Esau and discover how jealousy, hatred, and revenge can erupt within a family unit when members grasp for the wrong things in life.

This was the story of twin brothers, the younger of whom deceitfully sought a blessing (promotion) that was not rightfully his. What section of the Christian workplace has not experienced destructive actions by a worker who wanted a position of power and authority that was not rightfully his?

I find it tremendously encouraging to realize that God still holds to the premise that family members, responding to each other in love, will be the identification tag for His family, even though He knows of the potential for sibling rivalry. He knows His grace makes it possible to develop, restore, and protect relationships between members of His family—in your place of ministry.

Sibling Rivalry Among Jesus' Disciples

Among Jesus' own disciples, a competitive spirit developed when two disciples tried to obtain assurance from Jesus that they would enjoy preferred positions in heaven. The desire to take advantage of family relationships surfaced again when Judas found a way to prosper financially because of his intimate relationship with Jesus. Today, similar situations exist. Restoring and maintaining healthy relationships within the Christian family is a complex challenge. No simple formula will remove the potential of sibling rivalry, any more than one simple solution can resolve marital difficulties between husband and wife. The good news is that there are some excellent solutions for the problem of usury, and correcting that will alone do wonders in relationships between family members. Some solutions begin with us.

THREE

The Challenge Continues

During my early teens I was conscious of how our family lifestyle differed from that of others. My parents were devout Christians, committed to a fairly conservative and legalistic lifestyle. We had a precise list of do's and don'ts. I loved and respected my parents, but I really didn't like that list because part of it didn't seem to make sense. I recall going to a resort lake a few miles from home where there was a large outdoor roller-rink. The music was great. Those were the days of Ken Griffin at the Hammond—and Lenny Dee. The skaters had so much fun. But I was on the outside looking in. This happened to be one of the do-nots. I used to long for a lifestyle similar to that of my school friends. Theirs seemed better than mine. This is much like the children of Israel felt years ago. They looked at other nations and longed for a king. They didn't want to be different, even though God through His prophets had met their every need. They still yearned to be like other nations. They wanted a king and God granted their wish. They continued to learn lessons the hard way.

When considering how to develop and protect relationships within the Christian workplace, it occurred to me that some of the challenges I had witnessed were not exactly new. Members of God's family had similar experiences nearly 3,000 years ago.

My thoughts kept returning to Nehemiah. He was a wise man who feared God. Yet, he experienced some major confrontations from many of his workers. I wondered why.

The story is found in the Old Testament books of Ezra and Nehemiah. Please review with me some of the pertinent events told in this captivating account.

To the Bible scholars reading this book, let me assure you that I have no intention of trying to wax eloquent by presenting some new spiritual application of this well taught story. I present this story as a practical Biblical illustration of what happens when members of God's family work together, even under Godly leadership. This application requires a brief review of some real life facts.

The Israelites requested a king, and God granted their wish. They soon discovered that having a king wasn't everything they had anticipated. Later, as a result of their disobedience, God allowed them to be exiled to Babylon. Most of these Israelites were not ready for the culture shock of living in exile. In exile they remembered the "good old days" when they were conscious of God's protective care. Even in their rebellion they were conscious of how He held them as the "apple of His eye." (Deut. 32:10) They remembered the stories of how God delivered the children of Israel out of Egypt and led them into the Promised Land; how He had healed them in times of sickness and granted them continued victory in battle. But now they perceived that God had forsaken them as they suffered exile in Babylon.

Living in a country ruled by a people of different lifestyles and religions than they were accustomed to, they felt alone.

They didn't sense His presence as before. Their temple had been destroyed. There seemed no appropriate way to offer sacrifices and worship to God. Some of the Jews understandably lost heart. They became both angry and afraid because, when the future is unknown and all normal assurances of protection are gone, life can become scary. Many of the Israelites felt they had little left to live for. Some panicked and developed strategies for survival and prosperity in the anticipated absence of God's protection. They concluded that their best opportunity for success was to mingle and intermarry with the people of Babylon. Naturally, by doing this, they compromised their religious convictions and lifestyle. By making themselves more acceptable to their captors, they attained opportunity for financial success. Some of the Jews did not compromise their convictions. For them, life in exile was extremely difficult. Some eventually found it necessary to accept help from their more affluent brethren.

Each returned to Jerusalem seeking and expecting something different as a reward for their efforts!

The scene I have just described is significant in that this time spent in exile was much more than just a difficult period in their lives—these were life-shaping experiences. Personality and character were being molded.

Finally, by the decree of Cyrus, King of Persia, the Israelites were allowed to re-establish their own centers of worship, so they restored the temple in Jerusalem.

When Governor Nehemiah received his authorization to go to Jerusalem and rebuild the wall of the city, these brethren became his workers. Those, whose lives had been shaped during their many years in exile became Nehemiah's team—his family workers.

Some 50,000 Jews returned from exile, motivated by the desire to somehow recapture their heritage as God's people. God, in His faithfulness and mercy, gave them a fresh start.

Picture the scene.

The materialistic and self-centered joined together with the emotionally bruised and bewildered, and began to work on this project. Each returned to Jerusalem seeking and expecting something different as a reward for their efforts.

Nehemiah gathered the Israelites together for a pep talk. He held them spellbound as he painted a picture of a restored Jerusalem, complete with its temple of worship, and its strong wall of identity and protection. He helped them catch a vision that God had something better for them to do than live in exile and bondage. He reassured them that Jehovah was still their God and they were still His people.

That was all it took for God's family workplace to get started, because each pictured Nehemiah's vision through his or her own filter of expectations and couldn't wait to see their dreams and agendas fulfilled.

Nehemiah positioned segments of the Jewish family throughout the entire circumference of the wall building project and assigned work to each. The place was charged with enthusiasm!

This well organized project continued until the wall was about half built. This was an interesting juncture in the lives of many workers and, incidentally, it is a juncture that many reach today, when they accept assignments with others in ministry or Christian-type business.

The Halfway Point Crisis

Something happened at the halfway point of Nehemiah's wall building project that affected everyone.By this time

- ✦ Most had reached the place where the novelty of the project had worn off and all that remained was very hard work.
- ✦ They had been exposed to enough outside enemy ridicule that their emotions were on edge.
- ✦ They had worked with each other long enough to become conscious of each other's "humanness."

- Some had acquired a genuine resentment towards many of their Jewish brothers because of continued usury.

These relational elements made what was already hard work a whole lot harder.

Nehemiah was brought face to face with thousands of family members, who carried mixed bags of personal agendas and aspirations acquired during those years in exile. He was about to discover what can happen when family members seek to satisfy self-centered agendas at the expense of their brethren.

He was about to discover what can happen when family members seek to satisfy self-centered agendas at the expense of their brethren.

Nehemiah Identifies Usury

A large number of Jews reached a breaking point because of usury. The help they received from their brethren involved financial terms that were neither realistic nor just. They discovered that being close to the Jerusalem temple didn't make saints out of those in the workplace.

Not only were their hands bleeding and sore from working with heavy rock, but by now some had lost all of their earthly possessions or had heavy mortgages on everything they owned. Ironically, those holding their mortgages were Jewish brethren who had found a way to prosper while in exile. These had loaned their unfortunate Jewish brethren sufficient money to provide food for their families, but they assessed so much interest that eventually they took possession of their homes, vineyards, orchards, and even their children as payment.

These frustrated, angry family members sought help from Nehemiah. Listen to what they said to Nehemiah. (Chapter 5)

> "We have sons and daughters who have nothing to eat."
>
> "While we do this, others of our Jewish brethren are taking our farms and our grain."
>
> "We've had to mortgage our fields, vineyards, and our houses to get grain!"
>
> "Our flesh is as the flesh of our brothers, yet we are forcing our sons and daughters to become slaves!"

In essence they said, "Nehemiah, we know this ministry is important. We believe in what we're doing. We know that we are God's family, and that He is the true and living God. But we're losing our homes while we work long hours for this ministry. Even if we get the wall finished, we're as good as finished now! Everything we possessed that gave us security and pride has been taken from us by a brother. Is this really family? We believe this is where God wants us, but we feel trapped. What should we do?"

When Nehemiah heard this, he became angry. He gathered the nobles and officials together and said:

> What you are doing is not good. Should you not walk in the fear of our God because of the reproach of the nations, our enemies? Please, let us stop this usury! Restore now to them, even this day, their lands, their vineyards, their olive groves, and their houses, also the hundredth part of the money and the grain, the new wine, and the oil that you have charged them. (vv. 9-11, NKJV).

Nehemiah addressed the fact that within families, sometimes giving, not lending, is appropriate. Many Jewish family convictions were compromised during the exile experience in Babylon, which produced a greed and a lack of compassion that motivated them to even lend to their own family members with designs of greed.

Today's Family Workplace Is Somewhat Similar

Our challenge in protecting family relationships is actually quite similar to that experienced under Nehemiah's leadership. The sequence of events can be about the same.

Workers in ministry are in many ways a continuation of who they were before they joined!

First, something exciting usually transpires in the hearts of those who accept responsibilities in ministry type work. The tug of God's leading in ministry is always stimulating. However, after we've worked a while with our co-laborers in ministry we, like the Israelites, discover resistance to our efforts from those who ridicule and taunt us. We also observe the results of the years each family member lived in their own particular exile. Each spends considerable time interfacing with a social culture that is diametrically opposed to priorities of the Christian faith. Exile takes its toll. Even though most of those we associate with are members of God's family, each of us is a blend of lifestyle priorities and appetites acquired along the way. Workers in ministry are in many ways a continuation of who they were before they joined!

Try as we may to maintain a positive attitude, we each experience feelings of concern and disappointment when we acknowledge excessive elements of exile baggage that have entered the workplace.

I think most everyone in Christian ministry or business reaches a halfway point and must decide how to cope with this unexpected reality. Who hasn't expressed the sentiments that it's good to be with the Christian family but sometimes it seems impossible living up to the expectations we perceive coming from them?

Nehemiah Deals with Usury

Nehemiah commanded the Israelites to stop taking advantage of each other and to restore the lands, vineyards, and houses to their original owners. I believe this was probably the greatest miracle recorded in Scripture that related to God's dealings with the children of Israel: They were delivered from greed!

The People Did as Nehemiah Requested

Somehow, through Nehemiah's leadership, those helping in the project accepted the reality that back home under God's care, there was no more need to grasp or cling to material possessions. Through a revelation of the Spirit of God, they saw the significance of being members of God's family. As a result of their obedience, happiness returned to the workplace, and they finished the wall building project in record-breaking time.

I remember one particular ministry experience in which inequities were everywhere! So I cried out to my Nehemiah—but surprise! I didn't have a Nehemiah for a leader. That was a devastating experience. I admired this leader, but somehow failed to acknowledge that, in addition to his commitment to ministry, he was using this platform to advance his own materialistic objectives. I had listened to the Nehemiah pep talk and made a commitment of loyalty, only to discover the presence of unreasonable expectations.

When this occurs, we typically do a self-critique and ask, "What could I have done to avoid this disappointment?"

Scattered throughout this book you will find important keys to assist you in making wise workplace decisions. Had I known a few more of these keys then, I would have known how to protect this particular relationship and could have avoided disappointment. Fortunately, flags of caution surround this type of individual, if we will pause to recognize them.

Back to Nehemiah.

> *I think most everyone in Christian ministry reaches their own halfway point.*

It's important to note that this problem was not solved as a result of Nehemiah's initiative, even though he was a Godly man. Workers initiated the action. They confronted their leader. The time may come when you will need to do the same. When a situation develops where you can clearly identify the problem as being unreasonable expectations or usury, it's probably time to confront your leader or supervisor. Solutions will follow—but only if you have a Nehemiah for a leader or supervisor.

During the past thirty years I have visited with hundreds of God's family members who have been, or continue to be, part of the Christian workplace. Intertwined among stories of career fulfillment were accounts of how unrealistic expectations had taken a toll on their lives, families, and work relationships.

I don't want this to be your story too. Therefore, don't wait for things to be solved automatically by someone at the top. Many of the things that concern you will not automatically be resolved without a loving confrontation with a leader. Do so before the problem gets too big. One word of caution! Be alert to the identity flags of your supervisor or leader that indicate whether you'll be dealing with someone of Nehemiah's integrity and character. If you see too many flags of caution you may be wise to phase out of that particular work assignment, so you can preserve family relationships. Leaders or supervisors known to use or manipulate people are not Nehemiah's and are unlikely to correct problems involving workplace inequities. We'll help you identify the qualities in a leader that is most likely to resolve problems of usury.

FOUR

A "Family" In Transition

I'VE HEARD IT SAID THAT NO TWO CHILDREN HAVE THE SAME PARENTS. This statement is based on the fact that, although each new baby is birthed by the same two people, the parents may have changed in many ways since they had their last child. Perhaps they have grown wiser and matured, or their relationship as husband and wife may now be strained due to financial adversities. The home isn't the happy place it used to be. Things are different. Their lives are in transition.

Psychologists tell us that by analyzing a person's past they are able to predict many of the challenges to be faced in the future. How we respond to the challenges of life is determined by the decisions we make. Normally, our method for making decisions continues until, as a result of some crisis, we are convinced of the need for change. It's helpful for us to take an inward look at ourselves periodically, to discover just who we are, who we have become over the years. We may not be able to change who we are from a psychological aspect, but each member of God's family can become a person of good character and integrity.

Many years ago, before I entered the field of Christian radio, I became fascinated by a particular Christian entrepreneur. He had high energy, talent, charisma, and a mind for detail. We became good friends. I began to work with him. It was a great experience!

His organization was very small at the time. We were a closely-knit team, wherein each recognized the value of the other. It was obvious that I was as important to him as he was to me. I could have asked him for anything and to the best of his ability he would have made it happen. Knowing this, I did not ask.

We were two people within family—each expecting more from the other than either could give.

We all worked hard and God blessed our efforts. Success came. The organization became strong. I appreciated his commitment to ministry. However, in the excitement of growth, I refused to acknowledge aspects of change that disturbed me. It seemed the larger the organization grew, the more focused he became. He was in transition. It wasn't long before he had acquired all the characteristics of a successful entrepreneur (we deal with this in the next chapter). He saw only what he wished to achieve and not much else. This transition was painful for me and I soon was forced to acknowledge that our relationship would never again be what it used to be. I had observed the transition that sometimes accompanies success.

But I was in transition too.

With me it was different. I wanted to see God's blessing in the form of growth, but equally wanted our relationship to continue unaffected by change. I was expecting more from him than he could give. Conversely, he expected me to continue, enthused and excited about where he was going, as if that should be enough. That was more than I could give.

We were two people within family, each expecting more

from the other than either could give. We were two lives in transition. He was on his way becoming a big head, and I was on my way becoming a sore head. Success revealed some differences in us. It brought out the true entrepreneur in him, whereas I had learned years before that true organizational success occurs through the efforts of a motivated team. I therefore wanted to see members of the team succeed in sync with the organization.

In the preceding chapter we saw how character traits and lifestyle priorities acquired while in exile introduced tension and continued usury in Nehemiah's workplace. Unfortunately, usury is not permanently eliminated from the workplace with one confrontation. Developing and protecting relationships are an ongoing challenge, because every person continues as a life in transition, even within a ministry.

It is possible to transition from following a call to minister to that of following a professional career track.

Most of the challenges Nehemiah encountered were the result of decision processes developed during the Israelite's time in exile. For some white was white and black was black when it came to convictions. For these, disciplines were clearly defined. At times some of these legalists became disillusioned when they observed other family members enjoying a somewhat relaxed lifestyle because of their willingness to compromise a few of their convictions. Others, extremely weak in their convictions, compromised principles essential to the Jewish religion. For them black and white could easily blend into gray. They were determined to find a way to live that didn't hurt. Greed, lust, and immorality didn't look as sinful as before. They were each in transition, influenced by their environment. They entered Nehemiah's workplace, each possessing some Babylonian baggage that could impede relationships and work progress. Once there, the transition process continued.

Our Situation is Similar Today.

When I entered the Christian workplace in a pastoral capacity many years ago, I naively felt that the work of ministry would firmly establish me as a stalwart in the Kingdom of God. I knew I would increase my communications skills and gain knowledge of the Scripture through study and experience. However, I didn't even contemplate the possibility that, within the framework of ministry, I might allow ambition or material appetites to influence my decisions. It's a slow and subtle transition. I shudder to think how it eventually became possible for me to say to God, "I've left all to follow You. I've left a good career. Now, Father, how do I make ministry work for my benefit as well as yours?" A few of Jesus' disciples expressed similar sentiments.

It is possible to move from following a call to minister to that of following a professional career track.

In the ministry workplace this happens every day. It happens gradually. We are seldom conscious of change in ourselves. Others usually notice the transition before we do. If we are not becoming more like Christ, there is only one other option.

We live in a day when financial pressures are causing major transitions in ministry. While they enjoy their new and accommodating church facilities, some pastors occasionally look back longingly to the days when, in their old sanctuary, they had less restrictions on their ministry. Perhaps fresh in their memories is a recent board meeting where they were cautioned,

> "Pastor, with great passion you challenged your congregation about their giving, so that we could build this new sanctuary. We also incurred a heavy mortgage. Our suggestion is that, until we get this mortgage off our backs, you had better not offend anyone unnecessarily.

Of course, we want you to preach the Gospel, but please stay off abortion and politics!"

Some of these pressures can form a pastor into a professional theological diplomat. Similarly, Christian businessmen can change until they focus so much on their bottom line that finances determine many of their decisions regarding the books they publish, the products they sell, or the advertisements or radio programs they accept. When people change, organization and business philosophies also change.

When people change, organization and business philosophies also change.

It will be beneficial for us to look as some specific ways that Christians change within the ministry workplace.

The Transition Between Unselfishness and Greed

Each person enters the workplace with a certain amount of greed baggage. It's just part of our nature. Through the grace of God some eventually move away from greed to an attitude of unselfishness. In fact, the closer we walk with Christ the more we become like Him in this regard. Ironically, others devolve from moderate greed to more greed, within the very same workplace. In Nehemiah's situation God delivered those addicted to usury (a form of greed). It can happen today!

Jesus taught His disciples not to worry about the future. He drew an example from the lilies of the field that toiled not, yet were endowed with great beauty. He knew that if family members could only comprehend the immensity of His love and care, they would not be given to stress or worry. As long as greed is present in the workplace, some family members will feel used.

Jesus taught people to give and in so doing, discover the very heart of God who gave His only begotten Son. He taught this to a people whose nature was to keep rather than give. Nehemiah believed the Jews should be prepared to give and not just lend with exorbitant interest, especially within family.

Scanning my radio dial recently, I stopped at the voice of a pastor whose family was experiencing difficult times due to illness. His comments went something like this: "I'm so appreciative of those who have prayed for *me* during *my* time of stress and discouragement. You'll never know the load a *pastor* can experience during times like this. *I* need your continued prayer."

There wasn't the slightest reference to the discouragement and despair suffered by the other family members.

Often, if one brings even the slightest amount of selfish baggage into the ministry soon the inherent sacrifices of this vocation, coupled with the spotlight of attention, draws this unseemly characteristic to the surface.

The Transition Between Pride and Humility

The symptoms of pride usually surface in the form of sibling rivalry. As ministry organizations grow, it is natural for some to perceive themselves as being important keys to that growth. It is easy to forget that true ministry is accomplished through the work of the Spirit of God. God alone can speak to the heart of man.

Prideful people tend to expect more from others than what is reasonable or justified. They place relationships at risk through usury. Whenever our demands or expectations of others are unreasonable, relationships become broken and the work of ministry is impeded.

Jesus taught the disciples to choose seats at the lower end of the banquet table, not to strive for the better seats. By example, He left the throne of God and, humbling Himself, became man. He further reduced Himself by assuming the role of a servant, even going the way of the cross for you and me. He taught and lived the principle that, in the Kingdom of God, the way up often requires a willingness to walk a downward pathway, whenever needed.

When Christians are discouraged or when, for a variety of reasons, self-esteem reaches a low, there is an understandable temptation to clutch at position and power. Ours is a culture where people manipulate others and grasp opportunities that will position them above the rest.

The process of leaving pride behind can be a painful experience. Believe me, we are wise to move toward humility before He finds it necessary to bring us low.

The Transition Between Control and Servant-Hood

There is something in the heart of man that hungers to be in control. Life in exile has conditioned most of us with this appetite.

Jesus' teaching on leadership contrasts the grasping after power and control—so prevalent in our society. His philosophy of leadership involved a desire to serve, rather than to seek to control.

In his book about Christian leadership titled, *In the name of Jesus*, Henri J. M. Nouwen says, "It is not a leadership of power or control, but a leadership of powerlessness and humility in which the suffering servant of God, Jesus Christ, is made manifest." Again he says, "Much Christian leadership is exercised by people who do not know how to develop healthy, intimate relationships, and have opted for power and control instead."

We are safe in suggesting that most people in Christian leadership have been influenced to some degree by their secular counterparts and possess some inappropriate control baggage. A leader's very gifts entice him to peruse the current best sellers on the subject of leadership, and most of these reflect anything but the philosophy of servant leadership taught and lived by Jesus. About the only time I have seen people turn away from the need to control is when they come under the influence of a leader who has left the control baggage behind.

Those who are greedy weren't always greedy. Those who are humble weren't always humble. Those who are selfish, or who seek power or control, acquired those traits somewhere along their journey. Likewise, those who are generous and have discovered God's secret to happiness through servant leadership did so along the way.

Everyone is in Transition!

Let's take a look at the family members with whom you associate in your ministry or work.

- They are people of varied age, ranging from late teens through seniors.
- They have different skills, education, and experience.
- They have individual goals and needs.
- Many are professing Christians, but differ as to their church affiliations, and therefore have different standards as the foundation for their expectations.
- Those who are Christians are at different stages in their personal commitment to spiritual growth and maturity.
- They differ in their income, position, and supervisory authority.
- They have varied backgrounds. They bring their own separate baggage that must be handled in the process of spiritual and emotional growth. Some come from Christian homes, others from broken or agnostic backgrounds. Some were reared in poverty, while others may have been subjected to racial discrimination. Others enjoyed an upper middle-class lifestyle and educational opportunities. Some are in recovery from chemical addictions.

- Each one, either enjoys or wrestles with the complexities of the Christian workplace.
- Everyone changes with age, which allows each of us to view life from ever-changing perspectives.

During the past thirty years America has witnessed many Christian entrepreneurs whose beginnings were humble and team relationships close. God blesses this type of unity and hard work. However, who can predict how success will affect their attitude and priorities in future years? Who knows in advance how they will be influenced by an abundance of money and power? I heard a preacher on the radio yesterday say, "I don't care about walking on streets of gold when I get to Heaven. *I want gold NOW!*" When he was first called to the ministry, gold was certainly not his passion.

We're not in heaven yet!

Who knows in advance how they will respond to the changes caused by organizational growth? Radio, television, and the print media have enabled many small ministries to mushroom to national and international prominence. Some have handled this well: others have not.

Summary

If you want to develop and protect relationships within your ministry workplace, you need to enter it with your eyes wide open. We're not in heaven yet! As Dr. Jack Hayford suggests, the Christian workplace is not intended to be even the first phase of heaven. We are family members working together, and everyone needs some space for growth and change. When we adopt this type of perspective towards other workers in ministry, we not only benefit ourselves, but also become vital elements in maintaining workplace harmony.

Jesus told the story of two brothers. One, known to us as the prodigal son, squandered all that he had because of his lust for pleasure. Eventually he returned home, emotionally scarred, humiliated, and broke, because of his poor decisions. Being at home didn't end his problems, because he had an elder brother. The elder brother had remained at home to help in the family workplace, but unfortunately had become more cynical and self-righteous every day. When the younger brother returned and asked forgiveness from his father, the elder brother wanted no part of him. He was appalled that his younger brother had the nerve to come home and seek forgiveness after what he had done to his father. He was especially annoyed by all the fuss his father made over his brother's return. It seems strange how that he could live so close to his father for so many years without understanding his father's heart of love and grace.

We can either become cynical or participate in the joys of our Father. We have but two options!

We can do this too! We work in our respective ministries, attending to our Father's business every day. We can become professors of Greek and Hebrew, and put many chapters of Scripture to memory, and still not capture the essence of God's grace and forgiveness. Like the elder brother, we have but two choices: we can become cynical and self-righteous or we can humble ourselves and participate in the romance and joys of the Father's banquet hall.

The story of the prodigal son describes a family in transition.

I can only imagine the love and patience the father would need to guide these two siblings back into a loving relationship. This we do know: the father would never have welcomed the younger son home unless he knew he could love his two sons back into fellowship. Our heavenly Father utilizes this same type of love and patience to guide us into His banquet hall of forgiveness and joy. Sometimes we too put up quite a fuss getting there!

I'm Glad God's Love Never Changes!

Scripture records the phenomenal growth Jesus experienced in His ministry, a period of only about three years. There was no mass media or marketing consultants. People simply came. In just a few years Jesus attracted so much attention and acquired such great respect that some in government felt threatened. The love of God attracts like no other power on earth. The love and compassion of Jesus was a breath of fresh air to a people confused by the legalism of religiosity. Throughout His ministry, the quality of His love never wavered. None of the abuse He received from the angry and jealous mobs ever hindered the flow of His love.

Jesus Christ, the same, yesterday, today, and forever!

Jesus proved that a member of His family can be successful in ministry, achieve wide public acclaim, and also enjoy and protect family relationships. His secret, He lived what He taught on the hillside of Galilee.

Ministries Need This Same Stabilizing Presence of God's Love

Family members who radiate God's unchanging love are desperately needed in each ministry workplace. These workers become the keys that enable others to move beyond the symptoms of their own Babylonian culture into the joys of the Father.

Recently, I met with a consultant who had worked with a famed Christian leader. Though well educated, this leader continued to produce relational stumbling blocks within his workplace. I asked the consultant, "Why has no one close to him been a friend enough to help him see some of these things?"

The consultant responded, "He doesn't even see those around him who could be of great help. If he would only stop and receive some input from those who know him best, some wonderful things could happen."

This man came to the ministry workplace after having spent many years acquiring a self centered lifestyle in his own particular exile. Influenced by a member of God's family, he heard the call to follow Jesus. He obeyed. His intelligence and commitment guided him to organizational success, but he hasn't quite discovered one thing: when following Jesus, it's best to leave his egotistical baggage behind.

I think of another person, well known to thousands. His background was quite different. He had very little education: his parents were poor. His adolescence reflected a series of wrong decisions. One day he too had an encounter with Jesus through the influence of one who radiated God's love. It seemed easy for him to trust the provision of God's love—he had no reputation to uphold. With an unassuming attitude of gratefulness to God, he committed himself to ministry. Thousands have been attracted to Christ through his ministry.

Regardless of your particular background, and the personal challenges you face in your Christian walk, know this—if you are involved in ministry, whether as a volunteer, or a staff member in a Christian organization or business, you should consider yourself honored. You belong to a unique section of family, commissioned to tell about the marvelous grace of God. This can be accomplished only by those who have a passion to do so. That passion is found only within members of His family.

I've painted a picture of the types of family members Nehemiah had in his workplace, twenty-five hundred years ago. I have also described the workplace today. The good news is that these are the people Jesus uses to accomplish everything in His ministry! It's obvious that Jesus provides a lot more time and space for us to metamorphize into His likeness than we normally are willing to extend to each other. I believe we should remember that it is His ministry. Therefore, it seems appropriate for us to adopt His policy in regard to those who work with us in ministry. Hopefully, we will provide them with enough leeway in our expectations to allow for these ongoing transitions. By adjusting our expectations of other family members just a little lower, we may be able to share in the delight of the Father and, with Him, observe signs of spiritual growth and maturity in those we work with.

Within our respective workplaces we each continue to change. Babylonian type influences continue to exist both inside and outside the workplace. As in Nehemiah's day, we need to deal with usury- for the very same reasons: because of who we are, and the significance of the work we are called to do. We've retraced our family tree. Christians are members of God's family. The work He has called us to continue today includes telling the goodnews of the gospel to the poor, healing the brokenhearted, giving sight to the blind and freedom from suffering to the bruised. We lose authenticity and effectiveness in ministry to the extent we are either victims of usury, or as leaders, allow it to continue in the workplace. In spite of the affluence and technological advancements in America, millions today are lonely, frustrated and fearful, feeling empty and depressed. The hurting and bruised people we are called to reach are only able to trust ministries where the leaders and workers actively model the love of God. The elimination of usury is an essential part of this transition.

FIVE

The Christian Entrepreneur

PARENTS ARE OFTEN HEARD TO SAY, "I DON'T KNOW HOW TWO children can be so different. They live in the same home, receive the same love and care, but they are opposites!" In our families we try to make allowances for the personality differences in our children and help them each become the best of who they are. In the Christian workplace, we need to do the same.

During the past twenty-five years thousands of churches have been established in America, and some have enjoyed tremendous growth. Similarly, a multitude of Christian organizations sprang up to support worldwide ministry. Moreover, thousands of new businesses were launched that offer Christian-oriented products or services. Each such organization was probably started by a Christian entrepreneur or visionary.

At the focal point of most ministries or Christian-type businesses is an individual who envisions a job that must be done and believes that he or she is destined to lead that mission. To some it is a calling, to others a passion or vision. Either way, their lives are focused towards reaching goals they feel are inspired by God.

If we were to follow each major church denomination or Christian relief organization to its roots we would no doubt find an entrepreneurial vision and focus that gave it birth. Each experienced growth and the leadership mantle was eventually passed to an elder board, or board of directors. Change occurs in the lives of the volunteers and workers when the emphasis switches from the visionary selecting others to help fulfill one person's vision, to a board choosing a leader to help fulfill a collective vision. Each has a unique set of challenges in regard to ministry worker relationships. Because there is some visionary focus in all organizations we devote chapters 5 and 6 to discussing Christian entrepreneurs (visionaries), and the work environment they create. If your organization has matured beyond the entrepreneurial phase, parts of Chapter 5 may not precisely relate to your situation. You will easily recognize the information that most accurately applies to your ministry or business.

These chapters highlight the strengths and weaknesses of the entrepreneur or visionary. Their strengths are essential to the work of the ministry. Their weaknesses also become visible proportionate to their strengths. Entrepreneurs should especially be wise in regard to their own uniqueness, because strengths can lead to appetites that can eventually become weaknesses, in a Christian work environment.

It is essential that we devote significant space in this book to discuss our leaders. They are the ones who earn the respect of thousands through their leadership charisma, courage and energy. But some are called to work in the back-rooms of these ministries or Christian businesses, and with few exceptions, things look different from the inside. Actually, each Christian has his or her own back-room—that part of us that doesn't reflect the degree of righteousness or perfection we want others to see. On vacation last summer in Florida, I strolled by a men's shop. The window décor was distinctive in its simplicity. At the center of the window was an old rocking chair. Resting on the chair was a simple motto that read: "Help me to be the man my dog believes me to be". I thought to myself, I am thankful for my dog because he believes me to be the very best—at all times! He really enjoys being with me. When I'm in a bad mood, he doesn't judge me, instead he climbs to the back of the sofa and rests, just close enough to touch me. You couldn't convince him that there is a "back-room" to my life, where my behavior could ever be a disappointment to him.

It is no exaggeration to say that usury is usually present within organizations led by entrepreneurs.

With people, we're not that privileged. Those who know the back-rooms of our lives the best are members of our family. They know our strengths and our weaknesses. I'm sure it irritates them sometimes to have outsiders brag on us too much, when as family members, they know the "whole" story. In Christian leadership it's the same. We can't always be on stage, where our gifts shine the most. Behind the stage, is where members of our Christian family see us, and draw their conclusions as to who we really are. The greater an understanding family members have as to the passion that drives us, the easier it is for them to be tolerant when the back-rooms of our ministries are sometimes not up to par. We can never expect people to be as generous in their understanding and love as we enjoy from our dogs. But, as Christians, with God's help, we can reveal the identity of His family much better than we do.

It is no exaggeration to say that usury is usually present within organizations led by entrepreneurs, particularly when workers fail to take responsibility for their own decisions and let themselves be intimidated by their leaders.

During my career I have had the privilege of being closely associated with a number of successful entrepreneurs. I learned to love, respect, and admire each one. Their fields ranged from transportation to orchards. One was a pastor. A few were in broadcasting, and another was a successful Canadian politician. I have also studied employee life in many other entrepreneur-led businesses and organizations and have been fascinated by the predictability I found.

My observations are not those of a psychologist—I have not attempted a psychological analysis of any of these entrepreneur acquaintances for two good reasons: four are no longer with us (making testing rather difficult) and also because I want this book to reflect practical workplace observations. I desire to make it as easy as possible for you to identify the caution flags that can help protect relationships important to you.

Successful entrepreneurs, I concluded, are a breed unto themselves. The greater their success, the more they fit the mold. Thus, the best way to reduce some of the usury found in entrepreneurial workplaces is to understand the energy and focus therein.

Entrepreneurs—Who Are They?

Entrepreneurs are people who say, "It can be done!" and insist that it IS done!

I recall helping my pastor friend renovate his church. Replacing the carpet in the sanctuary, we first tackled the foyer area. Six of us ripped up the old carpet and created a roll about four feet high and twelve feet long. I don't know how much it weighed, but it was deadweight. It was getting late, perhaps about 6:30P.M. Only two of us were still there. Before wrapping things up for the evening, we tried to roll the old carpet out of the way, but it wouldn't budge. Finally, my pastor friend showed up.

> "Fellows before we go let's move this carpet out of the way!"

"Sorry," I replied, "It won't move. It weighs a ton!"
"No, we can do it, let's give it a try."

I'll never understand it. He didn't add much horsepower to the project. He probably only weighed about 140 pounds. But we moved it!

It's such a simple illustration that I'm almost embarrassed to mention it, but nearly twenty years have passed, and to this day, if I come face to face with a project that seems impossible, I think back to that huge roll of carpet that just couldn't be moved—but was.

Entrepreneurs have a way of motivating others to give far beyond their normal intentions!

Why was it that, just because the pastor arrived, we accomplished what had been impossible thirty minutes earlier?

I can think of a couple of reasons. First, I had messed with about all the dirty carpet I wanted to that day. Frankly, at that point, I didn't really care whether the carpet got moved that night or not. Perhaps I had reached my halfway point that particular day.

Second, the pastor had just come upon the scene. He was not sufficiently experienced in this line of work to know human limitations. To him, this was a new challenge. He merely looked and said, "We can do it!"

Entrepreneurs are like this. They focus on new challenges and believe they can be done. They have a way of motivating others to give far beyond their normal intentions. Their focus on achieving is so intense that it doesn't occur to them that something *cannot* be achieved. These true-to-the-mold tendencies develop and intensify in sync with the growth and success of their company or ministry organization.

Entrepreneurs: Some People Are—Some Aren't

I suppose there's a little entrepreneur in each of us. We experience times of yearning when our hearts begin to sing, "If I had the wings of an eagle, I'd fly..." and we envision ourselves escaping our hum-drum lives, free to do our own thing. Those who produce entrepreneurial "infomercials" for television capitalize on these yearnings and connect emotionally with the viewer's desire to be a "be-your-own-boss" entrepreneur. Unfortunately, about 75 percent of those who respond to these offers fail. Sometimes it involves the right person venturing into a business without adequate knowledge, training, and capital. But more often the motivation is wrong—that is, people respond to pitches like: "If they can do it, why can't you?" People can learn the disciplines required to lead or manage an organization, but growth requires focus, energy, courage, and vision. Not everyone is blessed with these particular gifts—entrepreneurship is not for everyone!

Many new ventures are started by people frustrated with their entrepreneurial boss. They mutter to themselves, "If he can be successful running a church or Christian-type business, then I surely can!"

Observing the insensitive or micro-management style of his entrepreneur employer and, perceiving himself as more relational, Ron sets out to prove he can reach his goals by being the opposite to what he has seen. He goes to the bank, withdraws his life savings, and launches his new venture. Once started, Ron takes time for everybody and thrives on the warm response from his workers. The workers think he's great! But, six months later, after a few meetings with his accountant, he discovers that, although he's impressed a lot of people with his relational skills, his venture is in trouble. The focus, energy, and charisma aren't there.

Many who assume leadership roles in ministry, or who direct Christian-type businesses, are what I call semi-entrepreneurs.

They lead, but they may be as much "manager" or "administrator" as they are entrepreneur. They find a way to blend their energy into a dual role. This type of leadership usually attains slower organizational growth.

Success in the Beginning

Successful entrepreneurs usually begin as leaders of close-knit teams. They provide energy and vision. Their small staffs know this and love it. This initial stage is exciting. Everyone pulls together. Each is appreciated and valued. Staff relations are about as good as they'll ever be! This closeness won't last forever, but no one really cares. They're all having too much fun! Working hard, but having fun. Team cohesiveness of this nature results in growth and change. Unfortunately, this type of change may be devastating to workers unwilling to adjust.

Change is Noticed by Workers Primarily in Two Ways

1. The entrepreneur's focus and energy begins to bypass the team, to focus on new challenges or goals outside the immediate workplace.

2. A new organizational structure eventually places some of the original team under the supervision of a staff minister, vice president,or department head rather than that of the entrepreneur.

Because of the relational bonding that developed in the initial stages of growth, this may be the beginning of the end for some. They discover that the close relationship they previously enjoyed with their leader has faded, never to return. Rapid growth can place some relationships at risk.

Eventually, entrepreneurial vision or passion may cause leaders to focus much of their attention "outside" the workplace, on people or things they consider essential to their success. As each new person comes under the entrepreneur's focus, some, inside the workplace will feel neglected. The desire to conquer and achieve, often exceeds the need to be perceived as warm and caring by those around them. This is why I suggest that success working for or with a Christian entrepreneur requires an understanding of the leader's unique drive and passion. Otherwise, some of the dynamics of growth may erroneously be perceived as usury.

Organizational dreams and expectations can become shattered when change is too severe. Near the end of this first phase of growth we discover that what may be interpreted as success for the leader, may not be success for the staff.

Traits of Successful Entrepreneurs

They have a narrow focus. Picture a mighty stallion with blinders on its bridle that prevent it from seeing to the right or the left—just straight ahead. MEET THE ENTREPRENEUR!

As a teenager I helped clear a lot of bush land with a team of horses. One of the horses was particularly nervous. If you walked alongside her she would jump. Or, if our dog happened along, the feet would fly. She became distracted at the slightest thing—until the blinders came. As a solution to the problem, my father purchased bridles with blinders for the horses. These prevented sideways vision. With the blinders in place it became a matter of "Why bother about things you can't see?" This is the way it often is with successful entrepreneurs because, to conquer or achieve, they must focus on their goal. They are straight-ahead people! This focus is extremely important to an organization's success, because, with their penchant for detail, they could otherwise waste a considerable amount of time trying to be relational with everyone around them, and opportunities for growth would be missed.

Many Christian entrepreneurs find themselves in a *Catch 22* dilemma. While their blinders allow them to focus on the goal, they eventually realize they've missed seeing the people who surround and support them in their ministry. Often, they are perceived as being uncaring and insensitive. It can really seem that way and sometimes they are. Remember the old song, "*You always hurt the one you love*"? The closer you are to a person, the more you tend to expect from that person. The result is hurt and disappointment. This is understandable in the workplace because, one of the main reasons you are "there" and not somewhere else is the entrepreneur at the helm. It is the leader that gives the organization identity. As an organization grows leaders do not necessarily become antisocial. The charm and charisma are still there, but are focused on people on the outside—those considered most important for continued growth and success.

Frequently the glue that holds workers in place is their love for God and ministry.

I think back over the hundreds of employment applicants I have interviewed. When I asked, "If we were to hire you, how much notice would you like to give your present employer?"

Too frequently the answer was, "Well, I suppose I should give two weeks, but even though I've been in my position for a considerable time, I could leave tomorrow, because I don't think my boss even remembers that I'm there!"

Being a Christian does not alter the entrepreneur's focus to achieve and conquer. Entrepreneurial focus is essential for growth, but sometimes disillusioned people follow in its wake. In fact, within the Christian workplace, frequently the glue that holds workers in place is their love for God and ministry. While this is good, entrepreneurs may choose to capitalize on this Calvary glue, and not ensure that workers are properly cared for.

Entrepreneurial initiative has enabled the Christian message to reach around the world. Food, medical aid, and education have all been made available to needy people as a result of this same energy and vision. However, when your garden hose is aimed only at your vegetables it usually misses the roses, because they are seldom both in the same line of focus. It's the same in the workplace.

Entrepreneurs Are Born to Conquer

Organizational growth affects people on the inside and outside!

Members of God's family are involved in ministries or businesses, similar to yours, that will be affected by the growth of your organization. It may be a church, Christian publishing house, compassion-type ministry, broadcasting company, or Christian bookstore. Those adversely affected may question your Christian integrity and motives. One church will accuse another of raiding their flock, a publishing company of overworking their authors, and broadcast companies of unfair competitive practices. Some practices can be correctly identified as usury but some are not.

Years ago the company I worked for had just purchased a fairly significant radio station. A broadcaster friend, whose company had been affected by our growth, approached me.

> "Don, I don't understand it, why did you have to choose this market? There are so many other cities you could have gone to."
>
> "What should a company do? Is it not right for it to grow?"
>
> "Of course, Don, they have to grow to stay alive, but why did you choose this city?"
>
> "What other cities would you suggest?"
>
> He named a couple of cities.
>
> "Those are good cities. Would you have approved of our expansion into either of those?"
>
> "Yes"
>
> "I believe there are a couple of Christian-formatted

stations there now. Let's see, your company is not in that market is it?

"No."

I laughed a little and said, "I understand."

My friend's reaction was entirely understandable. It's only natural to analyze the behavior of another from the simple perspective of how does it affect me? The growth and success of every Christian organization or business affects people inside (where the workers are) and outside (where the competition is). It seems too easy to forget that we're all family, that in reality we're all part of one great wall-building project!

Nehemiah made it very clear that relationships between members of the family of God were to be protected. In a very real sense, we are all working on the inside of the same wall. Thousands today, having been adversely affected by the success of another church, Christian organization, or company are crying usury! This is unfortunate, because Christians are not intended to be the enemy. They are family! If usury is present, it needs to stop so that relationships can be restored. If it is not usury, the process needs to be understood. I have concluded that what some consider usury may, in fact, be an inability or unwillingness to cope maturely with competitive issues within family.

The action Nehemiah took was not designed to eliminate entrepreneurial growth within the Family of God. He desired only to remove those elements that caused avoidable stress between family members.

Arrogance and Pride

I remember a comment made by a worker about his employer, the leader of a national broadcast ministry. "I wish he could be the same person when his mike is turned off as what he projects himself to be when it's on!"

Because of their unique package of strengths and weaknesses, entrepreneurs are wise to develop a system of accountability or support that will work for them. This is not easy for anyone, especially the entrepreneur, because their nature is to avoid counsel that might seem a deterrent to the achievement of their goals.

I lunched with the pastor of a church that has over ten thousand members. With a workday that starts at five and meetings and appointments that fill each day, this pastor emphasized that his top priority was his weekly meeting with his accountability group. These were men specifically chosen to provide accountability for him on any subject they considered important—personal and otherwise. I was impressed. A friend new him well and said to me, "Regardless how close you get to the man, his bubble doesn't burst. He lives his talk." How deceived we both felt when we later learned that those in his "accountability" group were little more than a carefully chosen "fan club". Incidentally, that story ended in tragedy.

I was impressed by his story because, the disciplines he described are contrary to the main characteristics of an entrepreneur's gifts. Entrepreneurs want to conquer new things—not deal with personal issues. In his arrogance he deceived many.

Several years ago I visited with another pastor and inquired as to the structure of his organization. He said, "Don, in my organization I have no one who can really create problems for me. My board consists of just me, my son, and an elderly lady that I haven't seen in years. I just send her papers to sign once a year. Other than that we seldom need to communicate."

His bubble had burst many years ago.

Probably no one is more susceptible to pride and a need to control than successful Christian entrepreneurs. I'm not suggesting that everyone needs to be part of an accountability group. I am suggesting that entrepreneurs need one or two persons in their life who have nothing to gain or lose by being candid and honest, including close friendships. One should not fault the alcoholic because of a desire for alcohol. They can be faulted though, if, when the desire becomes too great, they don't pick up the telephone and connect with a sponsor or friend who stands ready to help. Entrepreneurs know how to get the kind of help they need. They need our prayers, support, and encouragement in that which is right.

Entrepreneurs Have Great Courage!

They are willing to go beyond what is logical or reasonable to accomplish something they believe in. Nothing seems to stop them. They will move to the end of any limb, risk everything—go for broke! They have an amazing ability to envision whatever it is that they understand as being success and will not give up until they have achieved their goal.

When success is achieved others keep the branch from breaking!

Typically their focus and energy will drive them to success. Occasional failure would probably be the result of having inadequate information from which to make wise decisions. It's easy for them to seek too much information from the wrong people, and not enough from the right people. Some predetermine the kind of information they want and find somebody who will confirm their convictions. (There is always someone willing to tell them what they wish to hear.)

Courageous people tend to assess others by their own standards. From their perspective, people who don't have the courage to climb out on a limb are wimps, not really made of their same ilk. They frequently fail to acknowledge that the workers, whom they cannot see because of their "blinders", are the people who ensure that the "branch" they are on doesn't break.

Entrepreneurs require the assistance of people gifted in ways complementary to themselves. They possess only some of the many gifts that God distributed.

Admittedly, their gifts place them in visible leadership roles: however, each personality gift is significant and essential in God's eyes. Wise entrepreneurs will discover and acknowledge the special gifts possessed by each person and, wherever possible, allow those talents and abilities to flourish and become the value they were intended to be!

Winston Churchill said, "Those who can win a war well can rarely make a good peace, and those who can make a good peace never win wars."

In the Christian workplace both types are needed, those who can conquer and win new territory, and those who can preserve peace within the constituency.

Entrepreneurs Can Do it Themselves

At the startup stage of their new church, business, or organization, it's not uncommon to hear entrepreneurs say, "I'll do it myself if I have to!" This is not all bad, because in the beginning stages they may need to do many things themselves.

They will tackle whatever tasks they need to. They'll sweep the floors, empty the garbage, preach sermons, repair furniture, conduct weddings, make presentations, repair equipment, fill air-shifts, or counsel—whatever is needed. This willingness to do whatever it takes is what initially attracts many quality people to assist them in their ventures. It helps establish that initial team.

Normally, about the only time they can really do everything is in the organization's infancy. Chances are, if they are technically capable of doing too many things, they do not have the unique entrepreneurial gifts needed to drive success. If they are true entrepreneurs, they are not gifted with the patience needed to perform routine responsibilities on a regular basis.

I'll never forget attending a church service where it soon became evident the pastor was not pleased with his choir's lack of preparation. With a spark of irritation he cleared everyone off the platform. He picked up his guitar and continued—alone! He proved much more in that particular service than he had intended. He ruined the service, thoroughly embarrassed the platform workers, and exposed his impulsiveness and insensitivity to his congregation. It wasn't one of his better days.

The "I can do it by myself" attitude eventually creates problems. All Christian workers desire to make a difference. As mentioned earlier, to expect Christians to maintain a positive attitude without providing some release for their creative talent is a form of usury. It's expecting more than what is reasonable. Relationships are affected. Each member of family is blessed with talents and abilities useful in the Kingdom of God. Jesus recognized the uniqueness of each of His disciples, and he chose them because of their differences.

Entrepreneurs Have Energy Plus!

Perhaps the first real Christian entrepreneur I ever observed closely was a well known pastor in the Northwest who also became prominent on the political scene.

He lived an impossible schedule.

He produced a daily and weekly radio broadcast and pastored the largest church in his city. He was later encouraged to represent his city by entering the provincial race. People were so captivated by his positive attitude and endless energy that he was soon appointed Minister of Highways for the province of British Columbia. Each Monday morning Phil Gagliardi assumed his political responsibilities in Victoria, starting his workday early each morning. Evenings were filled with meetings and speaking engagements. Fridays he flew home. Saturdays he cared for church and local constituent responsibilities. Sundays he preached two or three services in his church. He was a man with a vision and had the energy of a dozen people—as long as he was doing what he felt was important to achieve his goals.

Have you noticed that entrepreneurs always have enough energy to do the things they want to do? Trying to interest them in something that happens to be outside their particular focus is usually impossible.

Successful entrepreneurs try to be on the cutting edge of whatever they are doing. It is not uncommon for entrepreneurs to get so caught up in the knowledge of where they're going that they can't understand why everyone else in the workplace doesn't show the same degree of cutting-edge excitement. This is usually because the workers don't know where the entrepreneur is leading them—they've never been told! No wrong intentions here, entrepreneurs are just too busy achieving goals to stop when we want them to and issue press releases. They don't realize that it's hard to get excited about a trip if you don't know the destination, and have no insight as to the benefits available when the goal is reached. Most people who volunteer for ministry, or who obtain positions within Christian organizations or businesses, are motivated to accomplish something of eternal value. They desire to share their leader's vision. To expect them to be excited and motivated without feeling a part of the leader's vision is expecting more than is reasonable or fair. It demoralizes. You could say that it's a form of usury.

Entrepreneurs Are Detail People

My entrepreneur friend in transportation was a classic example. He didn't start out in transportation. His first venture was a second-hand store, filled to the brim with anything he perceived to have resale value. He knew the price on every item in the store. He remembered where he bought it and how much he paid for it. He got into the transportation business because he needed a truck to haul items for his store. Soon he began hauling so much stuff that he added a second and a third truck. Before long he had a sizable fleet of trucks. Strangely, regardless how large his fleet grew, he could usually be found driving one of them. He never ceased having fun buying furniture, cars, antiques, tools, and the like, and he knew how to place a value on just about anything.

I've never known a successful entrepreneur who wasn't a fanatic for detail. They will spend hours trying to prove that a few pennies are falling through the cracks, or perhaps focus on some small detail within an organization. I'm sure you've seen them—or, maybe you're one of them! I'm convinced it's not so much they believe their business will fail as a result of misplaced pennies, as it is the satisfaction they get from proving a point. They will spare nothing to validate their convictions.

This ability to focus on detail is important in any organization. Normal daytime activities provide little time for detail focus by the workers. (The growth rate of most entrepreneurial organizations usually exceeds appropriate staffing by about a year or two). Therefore, these visits into the smallest detail can be of great value if it wasn't for the occasional flip side. The entrepreneur's motives can go beyond that of ensuring important items don't fall through the cracks. They frequently seek to validate their suspicion of worker incompetence. This could be a beneficial exercise if, after proving their point, they had the patience and sensitivity to deal with staff problems effectively. Do hard working people sometimes feel used as a result? Yes!

Entrepreneurs Are Creative People

Entrepreneurial minds are always busy trying to create some new and better avenue for success. Once they determine they need to solve a problem personally, earth will stand still before they'll accept the determinations of another. It seems they never get beyond the need to prove that it still takes them to do it, and frequently it does. However, it's hard for some visionaries to delegate and let go because, knowing their own skills, it is difficult for them to believe that anyone could do it as well as they can.

(Is it always that, or is it sometimes a fear that someone else could?)

I mentioned that, when I was a teenager, we used a team of horses to skid logs down our hillside property for processing. The best timber was at the farthest corner of the property. Leading to the timber was a narrow skid-road, probably charted first by our cows. (I hope at least one or two readers of this book will have spent enough time with cattle to know that a cow can't seem to walk in a straight line for more than about twenty feet.) Once I hitched the team to a load of logs, the twisty path wasn't wide enough for me to run alongside with the reigns so that I could guide the team to the bottom. The solution was to get them started down the trail and give them a shout of encouragement—and let them go! It didn't help my ego any but, by the time I eventually reached the bottom where we piled the logs for processing, the team was always there, patiently waiting for me to unhitch the load.

Somewhere here there's a lesson for entrepreneurs. "If I could trust my "horses" enough to let them do their thing, why can't entrepreneurs do the same with their workers?"

I can hear some visionary reply, "I'd be only too happy to delegate more if I could find a few people with some horse sense!"

Entrepreneurial success depends on two factors:

1. Entrepreneurial focus and vision.
2. The combined efforts of people who support that vision.

Wise is the entrepreneur who can release his workers to personal fulfillment and success!

They Are Intelligent People

Successful entrepreneurs are intelligent people, especially in their main area of expertise. It's fun observing their minds in operation. The more complicated a challenge, the more fascinating it is. This attitude can lead them miles from the simplicity of leadership taught throughout Scripture. A few actually reach a place where they see themselves appropriately seated at the head table of nearly every situation in life.

Jesus was undoubtedly the greatest entrepreneur the world has ever known. His disciples knew He was the leader. The crowds willingly followed Him. But never did He assume an attitude of aloofness from those for whom He would soon give His life. He shared with them the wisdom of selecting a seat at the lower end of the table. When Jesus taught this, He was referring to more than simply choosing a humble position at a banquet table. He was referring to the value and social safety found in possessing a humble attitude.

The Christian workplace presents a great challenge for successful entrepreneurs. On the one hand, their gifts can lead them to success. On the other, Jesus is their example as to how they should handle that success. They can easily be caught between the philosophy of their Leader and that of the Babylonian society in which they live.

Entrepreneurs Have High Self-Esteem

They have a tremendous belief in themselves, and there's nothing wrong with that. They are people of courage and confidence. In fact, Christian workers should each recognize that they too are of great value!

Eleanor Roosevelt is quoted as saying, "No one can make you feel inferior without your consent."

We are held in great value by God and He intends that members of His family are neither used, abused, or demeaned by others.

Jesus lived under tremendous pressure during His time of ministry. He had the challenge of preparing His motley group of disciples to represent the Kingdom of God following His departure to the Father. Even under this pressure and time constraint, Jesus was always approachable. He was always sensitive to the disciples' needs and concerns, as well as the needs of the multitude that followed Him. He knew the uniqueness of each of His disciples. He knew their hearts. He loved them and found ways to show it. He worked on building up the esteem of each member of His team by instilling confidence and trust in His leadership. No entrepreneur since has had a greater challenge than He did!

Entrepreneurs Have an Uncanny Sense of Value

Earlier I described my friend in transportation and his success in the buying and selling of antiques, furniture, and what-have-you. Successful entrepreneurs have this characteristic. Their interest in detail, coupled with the ability to remember detail, enables them to identify value.

Have you noticed they are usually more adept at determining the value of material things (tangible) than of people (intangible)—that is, unless people are the product from which direct profit is made, such as entertainment, sports, broadcast talent, authors, and the like. In valuing people, many use criteria similar to that used to value product items—buy for the lowest so they can obtain the highest return. This can certainly be usury! Therefore it is always important that we place a realistic value on ourselves and others.

Scripture records how Jesus healed a man who was blind. The story goes that He placed spit on the blind man's eyes and put His hands on him and asked, "What do you see?" The man replied, "I see people. They look like trees walking around." He prayed again, and the man saw clearly.

I don't believe God intends the Christian entrepreneur to see people as trees walking. Members of God's family are of greater significance than marketable commodities. God intends them to be recognized for their true value. If leaders would sincerely ask, I believe God will grant them 20-20 vision in this regard, so that their ability to value *family* will be as clear as their uncanny ability to value material *things*.

Entrepreneurs Have Great Charisma

Successful entrepreneurs usually radiate great charisma. Their people skills are an important part of their success. However, as I have mentioned, most of this charisma is focused *outside* the workplace. This is unlikely to change. Nevertheless, to the degree that workers understand the necessity of this outward focus, it becomes easier for them to lower their personal expectations of the entrepreneur, and thereby lessen the perception of usury.

Once you are part of the team you are no longer part of their dream!

As your church, organization, or business continues to grow, you may discover that your relationship with your leader is as good now as it will ever get. Visionaries need to be understood. They have a dream. From their perspective, the team is there to help them achieve their dream! Workers need to understand that—once they are part of the *team* they are no longer part of their *dream!*

I have tremendous love and respect for successful entrepreneurs. They are uniquely gifted people. Their gifts are of immense value to the Kingdom of God. Their focus provides vision and purpose for their organization.

Recently I visited with a young and talented executive who had been invited to accept a position with a large national ministry. His heart wanted him to say "yes." On the surface the opportunity seemed a logical step in his career. However, as he sought counsel from others in the organization, he heard one comment frequently: "Things change once you get inside." He wisely did not accept the position and continues to be revered by the leader of that particular organization.

Remember the Old Testament story of Naaman? We read that, "Naaman was a great man, but he was a leper." II Kings, Chapter 5, provides the account of this famous captain of the host of the King of Syria. He is described as being honorable and a mighty man of valor. But, he had leprosy. How many great Christian leaders of our time could we describe as being great men or women, people of courage and valor—but they are a ____________. These visionaries of our day are great and wonderful people. Sometimes, due to the nature of their gifts, they disappoint those who are more important to their success than they will ever acknowledge.

It is safe to say that in ministry organizations, or companies led by entrepreneurs, some valuable relationships are at risk. Focused leaders will seldom be able to satisfy the expectations of the workers who know them best. When workers understand the nature of an entrepreneur's gifts they can adjust their expectations so as to help protect these relationships, and not feel used. The rest is up to the entrepreneur.

God has made full provision for the needs of the Christian workplace. He made the fruit of His Spirit available to every life. Even entrepreneurs are not exempt from these provisions of love, joy, peace, goodness, and mercy. These can be nourished in any life that is willing. I recall discussing this once with a talented leader who quickly responded,

"But Don, I'm a type 'A'!"

I flipped over to Galations and laughingly replied, "You are absolutely right. It says right here that type 'A's are excluded."

Entrepreneurs are not forced into their leadership roles. They place themselves at the focal point of their organizations. They espouse their Christian business vision, or mission statement, with great clarity and passion. It seems appropriate, therefore, for them to remember:

> He who puts himself in the driver's seat of a Christian workplace knowingly assumes the responsibility to follow the example of his/her Leader—Jesus Christ!

Prior to His ascension to His father, Jesus singled Peter out for a one-on-one discussion. Much was at stake in this particular conversation. Peter was a visionary. He was an entrepreneur with leadership tendencies that could easily have matured into all the focused characteristics discussed in this chapter. Jesus knew this. He wanted Peter to maximize his unique abilities—without forsaking his real purpose in life. Because of who Peter was, and the significance of the work he was called to do, Jesus needed to ask Peter one essential question: "Do you love Me?" But why ask the same question three times? Because visionaries need to be asked three times! No other reason is sufficient to temper or season the controlling, power seeking drive, typical to entrepreneurs, than a personal commitment to love God with all their heart, soul and might. Jesus needed Peter to be the leader he was created to be—an entrepreneur. But Jesus did not want a day to go by without him hearing His heart-piercing words, "Peter, lovest thou Me more than these?" His challenge to every leader of a Christian ministry or business is the same today.

SIX

How to Maintain Relationships in an Entrepreneurial Environment

REMEMBER BACK TO WHEN YOU WERE A CHILD. DO YOU RECALL hearing your parents say, "You children must learn to play nicely together, so say you're sorry to each other, and play together like brothers (or sisters) should." For me it was hard to be made to say, "I'm sorry." It's usually easier to make up with people who are not family, because with them it's more of an optional thing. Relationships within family are different, in that family members don't stop being family. In the case of the family of God, Jesus said that members of His family relate to each other in love.

A friend told me recently, that while he really appreciated his pastor, inevitably when they would shake hands, or engage in a brief discussion following a morning service, his pastor always seemed to be looking *past him*, as if to see if there was someone more important to talk with. He explained that it wasn't like this when the church was small. He was both hurt and confused by this. The goal of seeking new families for a church, or clients for a business, can become such an obsession with the leader that sometimes the pursuit of these goals takes precedence over other relationships, including one's own family. It should not be, but it is understandable.

I empathized with my friend, because I knew how badly he felt. My friend thoroughly enjoyed his church when it was small, when his pastor had time just for him! But through the years it had grown, and now some things important to my friend had changed. He was struggling with this change. I encouraged him to discover some other people to shake hands with, who will make time especially for him.

I read a story many years ago (I believe it was in Reader's Digest) about a spectacular event in Beverly Hills attended by many Hollywood celebrities. A news journalist noticed that, in this crowd of motion picture personalities, an exceptionally large throng had developed around one particular individual. Naturally curious, he inquired as to who this popular personality was and discovered that it was comedienne, Phyllis Diller. While Miss Diller was certainly a celebrity, there were others in the room of greater notoriety. He asked why there was such a long line to meet her compared with the shorter lines for some of the others. He was told, "Miss Diller is a very unusual person; you do not get to visit with her long but when you do get to speak with her, she focuses her entire attention on you!"

People crave being acknowledged by those they respect. Although Miss Diller was an exceptionally busy person, she had not forgotten how important it was to acknowledge the people who appreciated her work. She remembered what many forget along the road to success. Many relational disappointments involve this type of change. Christian workers need to be seen, I mean really *seen*—by those in leadership!

Nehemiah discovered that the number one usury grievance he had to address involved financial inequities between many of the workers, the result of workers not being seen! Once this problem was corrected, unity was restored. To this day, whenever financial inequities exist, a ripple of frustration or neglect results that eventually reaches everyone in a church, organization, or business.

I make frequent references to the difference between *inside* and *outside.* I also refer to the *outward focus of interest and energy* that is typical of most successful entrepreneurs. The reason: this outward focus creates a void inside that becomes the birthplace of usury.

Many entrepreneurs lack effectiveness in this area in that, while they live to fulfill their calling, and love to achieve and conquer, they also want to maintain total control on the inside. Many want to control it all personally! When they eventually acknowledge the need for a number two person to handle the inside, too many seek someone willing to emulate them, and hopefully do things the way *they* would do. Or, in other words, become an entrepreneur's puppet. This fails to solve the problems of usury. There is an inside void that needs to be filled with someone possessing a different set of skills and personality traits to those of the leader!

A wise entrepreneur will find someone who understands people relationships, someone whose natural focus is on the inside (where the workers are) with less focus on the outside. The void should be filled with someone who will provide an umbrella of caring for the workers, one who is willing and able remove the inequities that impede organizational progress. This person will need to feel secure in his or her role, because a relationship of trust will develop between the workers and this person that may eventually be disturbing to the entrepreneur. While many entrepreneurs spend too little time developing warm workplace relationships, they can sometimes become a little distrustful of supervisors who enjoy workplace trust.

Knowing that many workers do not have the ideal supervisory covering, I have provided some tips to help workers protect themselves in matters of finances. Not all staff members within an organization will negotiate directly with the entrepreneur, but everyone, including volunteers, will find their work environment adversely affected by any serious inequities that exist between them and those above them on the organizational chart. Therefore, understanding the dynamics of our family enterprise helps everyone protect relationships important to them.

How to Negotiate Financial Arrangements

The presence of the ministry factor makes personal salary negotiations awkward for many, even though Scripture contains a multitude of references dealing with financial matters. That most ministry is performed on a voluntary basis adds to the confusion. Thus the question, "How much should I really get paid to do ministry?"

Relationships that survive the passing of time require a strong and stable foundation. In the Christian workplace, because of the family dynamic, equitable financial arrangements become an integral part of that foundation. Many are willing to accept employment in ministry for less remuneration than they need, or even believe is appropriate for their responsibilities. Those who do this often find their pathway filled with relational and attitude pot-holes.

Your First Meeting with the Entrepreneur

You will end your first discussion with the thought, "I'd just love to help or work for someone like this." This is to be expected, because entrepreneurs within Christian ministry are usually exciting people, who possess great charisma.

They have the ability to impress and charm. Because we are discussing finances, I'll take the liberty of giving this charisma a different name: communication skills—the "tools" of their trade.

These are people who have the ability to share their dream with you. They can articulate their vision in a way that makes you want to be part of it. They talk about wanting to make a difference. You say to yourself, "So do I!" They talk about God and their desire to serve Him. You say, "I feel that way too!" They speak with a passion that is both sincere and convincing. As they speak, you listen and observe a certain helplessness about them, as they articulate a task that is far bigger than they can handle. You can't help it but say to yourself, "I'd like to help!"

God uses entrepreneurs to motivate people in ministry. Not everyone can articulate a dream effectively. A technician would provide a set of statistics and charts proving a need for what the organization is doing. Managers would elaborate on the organizational structure that exists in order to achieve goals. The support staff would fill you in on all the behind-the-scenes work involved in making things happen, but the entrepreneur simply lifts you up into his or her vision and, before you realize it, has you tasting the excitement of being there.

Understand the *Tools* Used in Negotiations

Realize that entrepreneurs have their tools of the trade, and you have yours!

Perhaps what happened to a contractor friend will help explain what I mean. He was offered a contract to oversee the building of an apartment complex and was about to start the job, when a second opportunity was presented to him, that of overseeing the building of a new church facility. Martin was a Christian, and when his pastor offered him the job of building the new sanctuary, he became confused in the matter of finances. He was an excellent building contractor, but where ministry was involved, found negotiations difficult. Here's what happened.

First he attended a meeting with the pastor and a few board members, in which the pastor eloquently described the ministry potential of the proposed new church facility. It was an exciting plan. Let's sit in on the meeting. The pastor is speaking,

"You know, Martin, I am the pastor of this congregation and, I suppose, the one most seen, but when we get to heaven and God gives out rewards for faithfulness, there will be some surprised people. Many whose efforts are unseen by man will receive great eternal rewards. Like those who drive the Sunday School buses, or care for the children in the nursery. In fact, Martin, those who sacrifice time and money to help build our new church sanctuary will have a part in all the lives who will be touched through this ministry in years to come. I don't know how God keeps track, but I know He does. I wanted you to see these plans, Martin, because I'd like you to oversee the building of this facility. It could be one of the most eternally rewarding things you could do. Have you ever thought of it this way?"

"No, Pastor, I haven't. I'm just a builder working at my trade."

"Martin, we'd really like you to take this job. We believe God's work deserves the best and you're good! Naturally, being a church, we won't be able to pay you what you could get in your regular construction jobs, but we can pay you $ _____ a month for your oversight of this job, and will certainly give you a receipt for tax purposes, to acknowledge your sizable donation to the church. What do you think of the plans?

"They're great. It seems like you've thought of everything!"

A little later the pastor continued, "Well Martin, would you like to be a part of this?"

"Yes, I really would. I'd love to have a part in making this happen." He paused, "Financially though, it's going to be a real sacrifice, but the way you describe it, I guess I really can't lose, can I?"

To which the pastor replied, "Martin, there is no greater joy than that which comes from giving to God. This could be a turning point in your life."

The pastor used the tools of his trade effectively, but did Martin use his tools wisely?

Martin had recently experienced some unanticipated expenses at home. His family was desperately in need of money. The apartment complex job would have provided sufficient finances to get them entirely caught up. But after his visit with his pastor he felt guilty even entertaining the thought of turning down the church job.

With barely enough food on their table and with children badly needing clothes, Martin started to build the church. Two or three weeks into the project, his wife had some important issues to discuss with Martin, so she drove over to the job. As she entered the church parking lot she noticed a new luxury car parked near the work site. She whispered to her husband, "Who belongs to that gorgeous car?"

"Honey, it belongs to the pastor."

It's one thing to sacrifice when everyone is sacrificing but another thing altogether when there are *perceived* inequities within family. It took several years for Martin and his wife to work their way through the bitterness that resulted from being asked to sacrifice when, it appeared to them, the church was in a position to pay proper wages.

Within family relationships jealously or resentment can develop over a car, an expensive suit, a watch, or some jewelry. It doesn't take much to ignite resentments when one feels used. In this particular case my friend didn't know that the car the pastor was driving had been given to him as a gift. The car in no way reflected the church's financial position. Martin drew some very wrong and emotionally costly conclusions. It is mind-boggling to consider how much relational grief has been caused within ministries as a result of inaccurate assumptions by family members.

There would have been no problem had the church been willing to pay Martin proper wages or had Martin refused to work for less than proper wages.

That Martin felt caught in a spiritual guilt trap was technically his own responsibility. He could have avoided this trap by saying "no."

The pastor's car wasn't the problem. This was a case of *perceived* usury.

Martin had a choice. He didn't need to let another person's suggestion influence his decision. That he accepted the suggestion that God would reward him if he worked for sacrificial wages on this particular job was his call.

Martin should have had a dream of his own sufficient to help him make a wise decision for his family. His dream, admittedly, would be smaller in dimension than that of the pastor, but not of less importance. His dream should have been to provide for and protect his own family.

Seldom do people experience true success in a Christian workplace without taking responsibility for their own decisions. Otherwise, the blending of ministry and business results in confusion and perceived usury. In the final analysis, Martin took the church job because it was easier to trust the suggestions of the pastor than to get a handle on the ministry/business issue himself.

Millions of Americans observed a classic example of manipulation through guilt during the closing arguments by the defense in the O.J. Simpson murder trial. The jurors were asked to accept responsibility for national and social change. In his closing argument defense attorney Johnny Cochran challenged the jurors, "If you won't police the police, who will?" Implementing social change was not the jury's responsibility. This is an example of usury: Cochran asked more than was reasonable or fair of the jury. He used the burden of guilt to achieve his goal.

Participation in a Christian workplace can take many forms.

- Volunteers.
- Those who take part-time or full-time work, aware of the minimal pay structure, but pleased to do so, because they expect their employment only to provide a secondary income.
- Those who feel genuinely *called* to ministry to whom finances are far down the list in importance. They are entirely prepared to trust God to provide.
- Others accept employment in Christian-type organizations or businesses as part of their career path. What they do involves ministry, but their employment is needed to underwrite their family's present and future needs.
- Those who join ministry organizations where they solicit their own financial support to cover a predetermined salary level.

- Those who enter the Christian workplace knowing that, because of income from other sources, they are financially able to work for minimal income without jeopardizing their family's welfare.

All should realize that, whenever holy guilt is used in the negotiating process, everyone in that Christian ministry or workplace experiences the effects of usury directly or indirectly.

Entrepreneurs Are Initially Easy to Trust

Why do we continue to trust those who have not earned our trust in financial matters? We want to! Christians long to trust one another. It seems that many of us want so much to trust that we knowingly set ourselves up for disappointment and hurt. I realize that, within family relationships, if we don't have trust we have very little worth having, but trust can and must be earned.

It's naive to assume that when a person becomes a Christian he or she suddenly becomes Christ-like. We live with ourselves: we know better.

Years ago a giant of a man came to church. At the conclusion of the service, he accepted Christ as his Savior. He was so excited with the knowledge that he was a forgiven man that he said, "You know, God has given me eternal life. I've been a hit man for some Mafia connections for many years, but tonight, God has forgiven me. I thank God for this church, and I'd like to help in any way I can. Tell me, is there anybody that's bothering you these days? Just give me their names and I'll take care of them!"

Forgiven, but not quite Christ-like.

A sizable percentage of our population is approaching retirement age with little preparation. Many have experienced serious set backs. Disappointments, bankruptcy, divorce, bereavement, or serious illness have taken their toll. Their hearts long to hear words of hope and encouragement. TV infomercials that say, "You can do it too!" fill their hearts with hope. If they hear that same infomercial on a Christian-formatted TV or radio station, or read a similar ad in a Christian magazine, the trust factor increases tremendously. Why? They trust because it is Christian. If they hear a Christian say something that gives them hope they want so much to believe, that they often accept! By not insisting that trust be earned before they respond, they allow their hearts to run far in front of their heads, and often end up hurting badly and feeling used.

If a person applies for a position in the Christian workplace and the leader says, "There's no limit to what our people can make here," the tendency is to trust and probably draw some unrealistic conclusions as to what "no limit" really means. If he says, "Our company is small now, but if you stay with us and help it grow, you won't have anything to worry about financially," the tendency is to trust, even though these ambiguous statements mean absolutely nothing!

At a recent national convention I visited with a manager whose employer made what seemed an exceptionally attractive offer. His first reaction was to say, "If you're making me an offer, it sounds wonderful!" But this man was wise: instead he replied, "Thank you, I realize you have just thrown me a carrot!" He recognized the presence of an entrepreneur and his tool box.

We expect Christians to be truthful and not exaggerate. We expect them to mean what they say, and do not want to interpret their innuendos as techniques for implying something else. We expect them to be sensitive and caring. Not only do we expect them to do all of these things, we want to trust them. This makes us very vulnerable.

We need to pause here lest you draw the conclusion that visionaries, leaders with strong personalities, always take advantage of the other person's weakness. This is not necessarily true. When it does occur, they are not always at fault. Many workers in ministry are far too trusting in regard to financial matters, and subsequently fail to accept responsibility for their own decisions.

During my years in pastoral ministry I devoted considerable time to marriage counseling. Many stories I listened to were similar in nature-just different names and addresses. Allow me to combine hundreds of stories into one.

> They were married. The new husband was so excited with the love-of-his-life that he readily agreed to anything that would please her. He wanted love and peace, at almost any price. Confrontation was avoided—until, at that marital halfway point, the husband looked in the mirror, threw his shoulders back to look manly, and said, "I'm the man in this household!" Alas, this bombshell from heaven arrived almost too late. The scene changes. Fur begins to fly when mid-stream in the marriage the husband tries to regain his manly role, only to acknowledge that the capacity he now seeks had been given to his lovely bride, many years ago—by none other than himself.

Wise leadership can frequently eliminate relational problems in a workplace, through insight and anticipation, but only "you" know if you're feeling used. Nehemiah was a righteous leader-but he didn't call the meeting with his workers. He waited until they were ready to stand up for their own convictions. I believe what I've said is, "Don't blame the leader for sometimes extending his or her leadership into areas that are really yours-when, in fact, it was you who elected to trust them with some of your financial matters."As Christians, we each have our set of goals and priorities that influence how we use our respective tools. Who has not manipulated another with smooth talk? Was it to get what we wanted or what was best for the other party? What parent has not introduced God into a conversation to get some added help with discipline problems?

"Honey, you know that God is not pleased with you when you disobey your parents, don't you? You don't want God angry with you, do you, darling? He sees and hears everything we do!"

Everyone has been influenced by the priorities of our

Babylonian culture. It is therefore understandable that workplace motives will sometimes be pure and sometimes manipulative. To the extent our financial decisions are made in submission to holy guilt or manipulation, we will eventually acknowledge these inequities and make statements such as,

"I knew he was a Christian and thought I could trust him. I never even questioned the financial arrangements. I just knew he'd be fair with me."

"I wish you could have been with me at our meeting when we discussed finances. It was wonderful. When he shared his vision with me I felt so comfortable and safe. Had I known then what I know now, I never would have taken this ministry position!"

You'll want to cry out because of the usury but may discover that you don't work for a Nehemiah! Am I implying that the Christian workplace is filled with deception? Absolutely not! I am suggesting however, that the goals and agendas of both leaders and workers alike influence how they use their respective tools.

Entrepreneurs Can Be Disarming

Many have told me of their desire to work for various entrepreneurs. Typically, somewhere in the conversation they will say,

- "I'd really love to work for him. I know I could help him in so many ways."
- "She really needs what I can bring to the table!"
- "I know people say she is hard to work for, but I believe God may use me to help her change."

Who's kidding whom!

Entrepreneurs can be extremely engaging and often appear so helpless that one craves the opportunity to come aboard and help. We study these amazingly gifted people, observe their weaknesses, and somehow believe we can influence change.

Believe me, trying to change the person at the top is one of the most futile things a worker can expect to do. Don't think it will be different in your case. Over the past thirty years I've seen this record played too many times. If you decide to take the ministry opportunity offered, accept it based on the position itself, and not on some deep-seated secret challenge in human relations.

Consider your options carefully.

1. Decide not to take the work or ministry assignment, if you detect too many signs of manipulation or *usury.*
2. Accept the position if you feel God is leading you in this direction. Accept your visionary boss, just as he or she is. Accept the vision, and commit to support the goals every way you can. Accept the negotiated financial arrangement as being *your* decision—and be sure that it is!
3. Protect relationships within the family of God. Whatever you decide, try not to burn any bridges. This is God's family!

Entrepreneurs Are Great Negotiators

Once you've decided to join a Christian workplace, your financial arrangement will probably be the final item on the agenda. Negotiation is an important process—it not only decides your level of income but is also the occasion when the other party determines and acknowledges your anticipated value to the organization. So, let's talk about money!

Negotiating Your Salary

Six important points must be understood when you approach the negotiating table with your entrepreneur. You are in discussion with someone who

- Is a master at detail
- Is a good negotiator
- Understands value
- Likely has excellent communication skills
- Likes to conquer and achieve goals,
- Will probably use each of these skills in negotiating your salary.

The old saying that "good fences make good neighbors" is true! A clearly defined financial arrangement is like a fence that can safeguard important relationships. Do not leave the negotiating table feeling used.

Although an entrepreneur's capacity for details makes him or her a shrewd negotiator, he or she still enjoys the conquest. He or she wants you as part of the team! Use this knowledge to your advantage. Even though the entrepreneur negotiates your worth as though you were a tangible commodity, accept these comments as part of normal negotiations. Remember, this is the best opportunity you will ever have to establish your worth with this employer! You are still on the outside—what you say is heard.

It seems logical to assume that, when you are dealing with Christians, once the employer has had an opportunity to observe your work ethic, creativity, and skills salary increases and annual increments will occur automatically. This can be true if your organization is small enough that your leader really sees you. However, remember what we said about that *outside* focus? Remember what we said about the *blinders?* Accept the reality that after you have been in your new role for a few months, you are no longer in their direct focus. If you are not in their focus it is unlikely your earnings will be a high priority with them.

Think of a hunting dog that focuses on tracking a bird. Once the bird is captured, the dog shakes it a few times to ensure that it's under its control, and then drops it. Then, without giving the bird a second thought, the dog is ready to focus on the next prospect. The bird lies there forgotten. A little extreme, I admit, but the point is made.

Negotiating is a process most entrepreneurs enjoy. For you it may be a mortgage payment or clothes for your family: for them, it is an opportunity to persuade someone to join the team and help them achieve their goals. Whatever financial amount you agree on, will be an acknowledgment by both parties of your perceived worth to the organization. Unless you are comfortable with the outcome of your negotiations, it is better not to accept the position. If, for financial reasons, you feel compelled to accept the position on less than adequate terms, let doing so be *your* decision.

Salary Reviews

It is always wise to synchronize your requests for salary adjustments with an entrepreneur's request for added services. Your best time to negotiate salary is when the entrepreneur wants something. The worst time is when you want something. It is normally unwise to ask for a raise because of some personal need. Entrepreneurs are courageous individuals who go for broke for things they believe in. It is not unusual for them to consider a plea for compassion as an attempt to manipulate them. About the only chance for success in salary negotiations is proof of some fresh value you bring to the organization or business. Be sure your request is based on what your employer recognizes as value. Think in his or her terms, not yours.

If Not Successful in Your Negotiations . . .

Do you

1. Accept the employer's decision as being right and go on working?

2. Accept the employer's decision, knowing it was wrong, insensitive, and unreasonable, and continue working? (Can you do this and maintain a good attitude?)
3. Leave? (If this is your decision, try to protect family relationships.)

These are hard decisions, especially when we acknowledge that God desires that financial arrangements be equitable, because they involve His family. Ironically, expectations of fairness exist to a greater degree within the Christian workplace than otherwise. In the secular market one accepts the need to be alert to employment opportunities that lack credibility. In ministry or Christian business our expectation of fairness is understandably higher.

I recently corresponded with an extremely gifted person, who possesses great potential for ministry. He had again left a Christian workplace due to feelings of financial usury. I discovered that this pattern was consistent throughout his employment history. Each workplace experience ended with him feeling used, and angry. He burned his bridges after each job. There was no one Jesus encountered that He could not minister to at a later date because of attitude, regardless how He was treated! He always kept His ministry options open.

Can You Survive Without Compliments?

We all like to be appreciated and complimented for a job well done. Encouragement should be routine within a Christian organization. It's helpful to remember that an entrepreneur's focus on outside growth opportunities may affect the flow of deserved compliments. Compliments may be paid publicly for political reasons, but seldom personally or privately, where they really count.

Loyalty and integrity are taken for granted as basic expectations of those in a Christian workplace. However, because we all are in transition, character and relational qualities should never be taken for granted, any more than a husband and wife should assume that the qualities that make a marriage rich will always be there just because both are Christians. The outward focus of the entrepreneur never justifies a lack of appreciation to those in the workplace. It just makes it more explainable.

There was no one Jesus encountered that He could not minister to at a later date because of attitude.

I spent about fifteen years in secular broadcasting and personnel management. Ironically, the influences of my Christian faith were noticed and appreciated more openly there than experienced within Christian ministry or business environments. In secular broadcasting I was the one who was always sober on New Year's Day. My employers could depend on me. My language was always cleaner than the majority of staff. My work ethic was good, and, as a result, raises, promotions, and compliments came frequently.

Some Christian entrepreneurs feel justified in asking, "Why should an employer consider loyalty and integrity special? Why should it be necessary to encourage or compliment a person for minimal workplace expectations—aren't those qualities expected? We know only too well that integrity and a high work ethic don't come easy. Therefore, the characteristics of a true Christian lifestyle should be acknowledged and encouraged, because this does not just happen!

The question is, can we be happy without compliments or words of encouragement? This is possible, but only when the true source of our happiness and fulfillment comes from God.

How Is Your Self-Esteem?

Isn't it enough to know that you are doing a good job? For entrepreneurs it is. Who encourages them? Their personal vision keeps them motivated. For them, achieving is good enough.

Is it possible for volunteer workers in a ministry, or employees of Christian-type companies, to consider a job well done to be a reward in itself?

I believe the answer should be *yes!*

It is easy to be so focused on the activities or reactions of charismatic leaders that everything they do, or do not do, seems to affect us. This shouldn't be. We should never become so consumed by our leaders, that we forget that we too have a life of equal importance to theirs! We should always respect leaders, but never idolize them. It is possible to become so immersed in their activities that the slightest disappointment in this relationship affects our sense of fulfillment. Try to keep work or ministry activities in proper balance with life outside the workplace. This includes our families, social life, music, sports, education, goals, golf, and dreams. Keep enough of your life under your control that you enjoy a healthy sense of accomplishment, regardless of what happens in the workplace. Start setting your own goals on and off the job. On the job, enjoy great satisfaction from each accomplishment. Off the job, do the same.

How Do You Handle the Little Things?

Caring for details is a major key to an entrepreneurs' success. It is not unusual for them to perceive carelessness in detail as a character flaw. Knowing this, be punctual and attentive to the little things. Be meticulously honest in financial matters. If you are terminated it will probably relate to some relatively minor issue that is interpreted as a lack of integrity.

How Is Your Image with the Leader?

Successful entrepreneurs take risks. They go out on a limb for things they believe. Even though their success depends on people who are not strong in entrepreneurial characteristics, they are attracted to those who have this same out-on-a-limb courage.

> *The more you acknowledge your own out-on-a-limb strengths the more you will avoid being intimidated by the visionary.*

This need not discourage you because you also are a risk taker! You may never have launched a new company or felt called to start a new church or organization, but you may have high levels of courage in other areas. These are important—if not to them, to you! What about the time you entered a regional competition as a soloist, and performed before thousands? Or the recent boat trip you took down the rapids, or when you skied down some precarious run. Perhaps as a parent you have taken a tough love approach within your own family that placed family relationships at risk.

The more you acknowledge your own out-on-a-limb strengths the more you will avoid being intimidated by the entrepreneur. Visionaries detect fear. People with low self-esteem show fear, usually by being defensive. Therefore, it helps for you to consider your own strengths and let your attitude reflect this assurance. Believe me, an attitude of confidence and assurance will be noticed.

How Important is Having Your Own Turf?

My philosophy is that a person who *builds* a house has the right to pound nails wherever he or she wants. This understanding has enabled me to enjoy success in various entrepreneurial environments. I simply do not expect it to be otherwise.

You have a job description and perhaps an organizational chart indicating supervisory relationships. Please, do not cling to this, because entrepreneurial leaders do not have the time or patience to obtain information or give instructions via that chart, even if they created it. Being a Christian does not destroy natural entrepreneurial tendencies. With entrepreneurs time is important. They go directly to whomever they desire, as frequently as they desire, for information. They give instructions to anyone they please, and while it frustrates the dickens out of those in management, it's their "house" and they can pound nails wherever they want to! They frequently leave a mess, and a lot of nail holes, but those can usually be filled up and smoothed over by people like you and me. That's why we are valuable to them—they really do not know how to clean up most of the messes they make.

It's futile trying to change this. You cannot! Learn to live with it and be happy.

Be flexible—or you probably will not last.

I attended an Alanon stag meeting in Orange County. Alanon is a support organization that helps people cope with alcoholic or other addictive situations they must deal with on the job or in their homes. At the end of this meeting I was asked if I had anything to say. I said, "I'm rather disappointed. I came seeking information as to how I could help curb the addictive behavior of a friend, but have not received the help I sought. All I've heard are some suggestions as to how to survive the relationship with minimal stress on me."

The fellows applauded, saying, "Excellent, Don, you've got it!"

I frequently breathe the short prayer of serenity: "Dear God, help me to change the things I can and accept the things I cannot change, and grant me the wisdom to know the difference."

This prayer works just as appropriately in an entrepreneurial workplace as it does at an AA meeting.

How Is Your Attitude?

Hopefully, you have a "great" leader, whose positive and encouraging attitude permeates your entire work environment. This was and is God's intention. He has given us the ability to choose. Every person within your ministry, from the top down, or bottom up, can choose a positive attitude.

If your workplace occasionally becomes a disappointment to you (and it may) it will take courage and faith to maintain a good attitude, especially if it has to start with you. Try to remember that, in the Christian workplace, a positive attitude is essential if only for *you*!

The Importance of a Positive Attitude

- ♦ To remove usury we must be able to interact successfully with others in the workplace. This requires a positive attitude.
- ♦ Acquiring an understanding of others in the workplace can eliminate some usury. A positive attitude provides the mental clarity needed to understand the other person.
- ♦ The elimination of some forms of perceived usury requires lowering our expectations of others. Only those with a positive attitude can do this adequately.
- ♦ A positive attitude enables you to earn the respect of others. People seldom try to use those they respect.

Each sector of the Christian workplace has its own culture. Each Christian leader/entrepreneur is at a different place in his or her relationship with Jesus Christ. Therefore, the concerns mentioned in this and the preceding chapter will apply in varying degrees to each ministry or business. The more Godly the leader, the better the worker relationships, and the lesser the chance for continued usury!

The Mantle of Authority Will Eventually Pass to Another

Typically, ministries, or businesses launched by entrepreneurs or visionaries, will move into a more operational mode when the leader passes the mantle of authority to a successor or board of directors. This normally occurs within the first twenty to twenty-five years. The mission statement may remain unchanged, but the emphasis or passion reflects the personality of a board that employs a leader to fulfill its combined desires.

We really need some more Nehemiahs!

Possibly your ministry or organization has already transformed into this second phase of maturity, and you've never experienced the loneliness and frustration that occurs within the void caused by an entrepreneur's outward focus. While your work or ministry environment may be less stressful in some ways an organization that lacks a strong outward focus usually develops its own set of relational problems. Personality conflicts or agendas frequently develop within the board (sibling rivalry), and the absence of a clearly defined mission, creates worker frustration.

Our mission has some unique relational risks, but the importance of the task makes it all worthwhile. As members of God's family, we accept the challenge!

SEVEN

Elements that Can Destroy

OURS IS A SMALL FAMILY. I HAVE OFTEN ENVIED LARGE FAMILIES where brothers and sisters live close enough to each other that they can easily socialize, where cousins become important to each other, and grandparents add stability to the lives of their grandchildren. I expressed these sentiments to a friend recently who has lived life surrounded by family and relatives. He replied, "You're right, Don. Sometimes it's great being close to family and relatives, but sometimes I wish I was miles away! Have you considered that maybe you're the lucky one?"

◆

I'll never forget a friend I met in church about twenty years ago. That he was an African-American gives my story special meaning. We became very good friends. Thomas was about six foot three, and was physically very strong, hindered only by some shrapnel wounds received during combat in World War 2. I recall a particular conversation with him,

"Don, I've never quite been able to figure the difference between how it used to be during the war and how it was when I returned home to America. Overseas, in the foxholes, I was everybody's friend. But later, when we returned home to America, those same people didn't know I existed. When we were in the thick of the battle, and soldiers were getting hit right and left in their foxholes by exploding bombs and aircraft fire, the fellows would shout, Thomas, can you help get Harry, he's been hit! You see, Don, I was the strongest soldier in my platoon, and it took a lot of strength to carry a wounded soldier into safety. Trying to carry a badly wounded soldier from where he got hit to the first aid tent was hard. You had to do it while stooping over so as not to get hit yourself. As long as the enemy bombs were dropping, I was everybody's buddy. I risked my life dozens of times, leaving the safety of my own foxhole to try to help somebody. Because I was big and strong didn't mean I wasn't scared. Believe me, I was just as scared as anybody. But somebody had to do it so I did. It was the right thing to do. Eventually, I got hit myself trying to bring a soldier in."

Then he paused, and looked down with a sad and bewildered expression on his face.

"What I don't understand, Don, is the moment the war was over and we got on the ship heading back to America, nobody even remembered my name. It hurt more than I can ever tell you. I saved the lives of dozens of their buddies, but there were no slaps on the back to say thank you for risking your life for my friend. They just didn't know me. I was their hero when the bombs were dropping, but back on that ship heading home I was friendless. If only *one person* would have said thank you it would have been worth it. Don, what was the difference? I was the same person on the ship as I was on the battlefield!"

I don't know how you would have answered him. Naturally, we discussed many of the issues involved. It seemed the best thing I could do was to simply be his friend in peacetime. He was a good friend. Unfortunately, though, he carried those wartime hurts with him till he died.

There is something about family that seems to need an enemy in order to survive. If there isn't a clearly defined enemy outside, family creates one inside. I have a pastor friend who understands this. Every Sunday he does his best to get his people shouting mad at the devil. He discovered that if you can keep family members focused on an enemy, they won't start shouting at each other. As long as a family can see enemy bullets flying around, relationships seem to be fine. Family members need a vision, they need a cause, something to keep them focused, or they tend to self-destruct.

There is something about family that needs an enemy in order to survive.

Winston Churchill was a master at keeping his family focused on the *real* enemy. In one speech he said, "Dictators ride to and fro upon tigers which they dare not dismount. And the tigers are getting hungry."

John Kennedy mastered the art of keeping his American family focused on the real enemy. "We are not lulled by the momentary calm of the sea or the somewhat clearer skies about. We know the turbulence that lies below, and the storms that are beyond the horizon this year. But now the winds of change appear to be blowing more strongly than ever, in the world of communism as well as our own."

These two great leaders knew the importance of keeping their countrymen focused on the enemy and would use descriptive, creative analogies to ensure they were understood.

God created man with a need to be productive. The apostle Paul admonished the family of God to *press towards the mark of the high calling of God in Christ Jesus.* He knew the importance of keeping the family of God focused.

I have never known an organization or company that didn't experience some slack periods. These always occurred when the focus or challenge was not clearly defined. In Nehemiah's workplace, the lull came when some were suspicious that the enemy had infiltrated their own workplace. They had lost their focus. It was in this climate of frustration and confusion that the problem of usury climaxed. Fear gripped the hearts of the Israelites. It was only after the usury matter was properly dealt with that family members discovered that the real enemies were still on the outside of the wall. Similarly today, during times of confusion, leaders can erroneously identify workers as being the enemy, only to discover that a lack of momentum in their organization is the root cause of the confusion.

I used to enjoy trolling for salmon along the southern coast of British Columbia. Trolling was always best during one of the mean tides. When the tide reached either its highest or lowest level, for about a two-hour period the channel could become as placid as a lake. During those periods when the ocean currents were neither going out nor coming in, shrimp would rise to the surface. This made excellent feeding for the salmon and excellent trolling for anglers. Ministries and Christian businesses likewise experience their own mean tides, when there is no visible movement or focus within their organizations. During these periods many things previously unseen rise to the surface and become visible. (I'm not referring to shrimp.) The absence of the current (leadership passion), which keeps family members focused in one direction, provides opportunity for problems to surface that otherwise would remain unnoticed.

This speaks to the importance of keeping purpose in our lives, companies, and ministry organizations. Not only is it essential that we be ever mindful of the identity of our true enemy, but also that we retain a passion in regard to our goals and purpose in ministry. Churches and Christian businesses that are successful in keeping focus or momentum in their organizations, enjoy the fruits of true and fulfilling success.

Dealing with Enemies on the Inside

The entrance of Christ into one's life makes a tremendous difference! In fact, it soon becomes evident that the newly adopted priorities and lifestyle of Christianity run contrary to most social trends. Christians commit to the highest standard of moral and relational values on earth. We dedicate ourselves to running the race in response to the high calling of our Leader, Jesus Christ. Life takes on a whole new dimension when we accept His offer of grace and forgiveness. The greater our grasp of the "family" to which we now belong, the easier it is to accept the reality of the dynamics of family life, such as sibling rivalry, that occurs between family members.

When family members lose sight of the importance of the work they are doing, energy seems to dissipate in many directions. It is at this juncture that usury within Christian organizations is felt the most, and when both real and perceived usury is exaggerated out of proportion.

A few months ago I received a mailing from a party who has conducted a Christian family vendetta for over a year, and there are no signs of closure yet. Last evening I spoke with a pastor who devotes his life to further the cause of Christ in his community, while within his own organization he is being attacked relentlessly by one or two family members on the church board. I received a fax defaming another family member, the continuation of a vendetta that is now in its second year. We can only guess at the hundreds of hours that have been diverted from the important wall-building project because of these three situations alone. Family members became either the aggressor or respondent in these tragedies. Each involved family members imposing demands on others that were not reasonable. Each was a situation where the principle accusers lost clarity as to who or what was the real enemy. They lost sight of the importance of who they were as members of God's family, and also the significance of the work they were called to do. Their destructive vendettas emerged from personal agendas, that had no legitimate place in Christian ministry.

The removal of usury begins when individuals of conviction denounce it first within their own sphere of influence. It is not in anyone's power to remove it all, but each person can remove some that is real, and some that is perceived to be real.

When identifying our true enemies, sometimes our perceptions are correct, but sometimes they are not.

I attended a seminar along with several hundred pastors and church leaders. Mid-morning the speaker gave an opportunity for a refreshment break, and everyone quickly moved to an outside area for some coffee, and some other refreshments. I headed for the washrooms. I determined which was for me, and was soon inside a spacious facility standing face to face with a middle-aged lady. I thought to myself, "Madam, how embarrassed you must feel, don't you realize that you're in the men's washroom?" I'm sure she was thinking, "You foolish man, don't you know where you are?"

We each perceived ourselves to be right, but one of us was wrong!

I paused, and looked around for some plumbing fixtures appropriate to men's washrooms, but there were none! I was forced to face a moment of truth. My perceptions were in error! My real problem was how do I get out of here without being noticed?

We will never bat 100 percent accuracy in our perceptions in regarding our enemies. When we become discouraged or confused, we tend to concentrate on ourselves and how we are feeling, and are ready to identify almost anything or anyone who comes into our pathway as being the enemy. When our vision is blurred in this way, we can make some tragic relational mistakes.

It is up to each of us to eliminate whatever usury we can from our place of work. We can accomplish this only to the extent that we

- ♦ Consider our work in ministry of sufficient importance to justify preserving healthy family relationships.
- ♦ Consider our identity as members of God's family of

sufficient importance to justify removing inequities that cause unnecessary relational stress.

This awareness will help ensure that we check our own motives before we suspect other family members of being the real enemy. There *is* a real enemy!

Bolstering a ministry's relational immune system requires that we address a multitude of little things. You've probably noticed that within a family even little things can become quite significant. A single red rose can bring extreme happiness between members of a family, and a single negative comment can be equally devastating. During slack times in our lives or organizations, a combination of minor forms of usury rise to the surface that can prove extremely destructive. We should consider a few examples.

Personal Hurts Can Develop into a Form of Usury

A national ministry has used magazine classifieds for years to develop its mailing list. Their ad asks a few simple questions, including, "Do you feel misunderstood?" Of the ten options provided for the reader's response, this one is checked the most.

Misunderstandings frequently occur within families, probably because the closeness of our relationships provides us with sufficient confidence to judge, not only the other person's actions, but also their motives.

Parents expect their children to clearly understand and follow orders. Children similarly expect parents to understand the reasons for their behavior at each stage of growth. If you feel misunderstood today, chances are it involves some member of family. Unless addressed appropriately, misunderstandings can evolve into hurt, discouraged people. Hurting people usually expect a little too much from others, which can lead to what I would call a form of usury. It is ironical how in about every ministry staff there is one lovely, sensitive Christian who always has some special hurt or discouragement to deal with. Some people seem to possess a magnetic force that brings them in contact with relational circumstances that nurture hurt.

Hurts within ministries usually fall into one of three categories

- Unrealistic expectations of other workers or leaders
- Struggles related to control or power
- A loss such as bereavement, divorce, financial loss, or the like that comes unannounced.

UnAnnounced Hurts

Some hurts are impossible to avoid. They are a part of life itself. Every year, in the midst of our happiness, we have to let go of something or somebody precious. When this happens, we hurt! For me, when the unavoidable comes, it helps if I can give emotional release to this pain as quickly as possible. I couldn't always do this.

In my younger years I was taught that it was unmanly to show emotion. Men did not cry. I can remember vividly when my mother passed away. As a 25-year-old I stood beside my mother's casket at the funeral service and sang, *"Over in glory we'll not shed a tear, no disappointment, no heartache, no fear."* Tragically, I wasn't able to shed a tear then, let alone in eternity! It was several weeks after my mother died before I was able to experience a release to the hurt and pain I suffered through her passing. I did that in private. One should give release to unavoidable hurt, if one is lucky enough to know how to cry. I wish I could have learned the art of release earlier in life.

Hopefully, people who suffer hurt or discouragement as a result of unavoidable circumstances will seek help from their pastor or, Christian psychologist/counselor. One should not try to struggle alone too long.

Family members in a Christian workplace are sensitive to

those who hurt. They will listen, be understanding, and empathize. It's a part of who we are as Christians! However, there comes a time when the empathizers desire to move beyond nursing the hurts of a co-worker, especially when the situation is dragging out like a soap opera on TV. The truth is, no one enjoys working along side of hurting people, who are usually so consumed with their hurts that their conversation is focused solely on their problems. If not released from this obligation in a reasonable time, relationships become strained. Chronically hurting people often require much more attention from others than is reasonable. I call it usury.

Control and Power Struggles Can Cause hurts

Those who know my wife, Nikki, and me well would probably enjoy riding in the back seat of our car sometime as we navigate the freeway. If I am behind the wheel it goes something like this,

> "Don, you're not going to let that little old Toyota pass you, are you?" "Don, you're letting *everything* pass you!"
>
> Then she gestures with her hands and says, "Get over in this lane, get by them, they can't do that to us!"
>
> Later, rather disgustedly, "Don, I don't believe it, look at that beat up old car going right by us and you don't do anything about it! Don't you see it?"
>
> Then it's my turn, "Honey, my philosophy is this. I determine how fast I want to drive and will not allow a Toyota, Ford, or twenty-year old car control my speed, regardless how many lanes are open. I'm doing 70. That's the speed I want to drive, not the speed I have to drive in order to pass that old Toyota"
>
> Then, when I think she has given up and is not watching, I will shift over a couple of lanes, and pass a few cars. But to be sure, she has noticed and says, "Go

> Don Go! Go Don Go! What a maneuver!"
>
> When Nikki's behind the wheel, she'll probably hear me say, "Honey, do you have to pass everything on the road. Are you competing with the entire world?"
>
> "Have I ever had an accident?" she responds.
>
> Silence. (She is a very good driver.) At this point I feel obligated to wax philosophical and say, "You know, it's so easy for us to be controlled by what others do. The clothes we buy, the kind of house we live in. We need to learn to be *free* and determine our own course in life. The Toyotas and Fords of this life should not control our lives."

By this time it seems wise for me to shut up or change the subject.

It would be so much easier for me to simply drive according to her comments and gestures, but then, I would not be doing the driving. I would be letting outside circumstances govern my day—and to me, that is not freedom on the freeway. You know where I'm going with this. I'm describing the controlling influences of the freeway but what about those controlling influences in your part of your ministry.

To some degree we are all controlled by the Toyotas of life, and usually resent them. Think of how many times in your work or ministry somebody appears alongside and tries to pull in front of you. In fact, much of the conflict within the Christian workplace involves one family member imposing a particular course of action on another, pulling in front with his or her way of doing things. If the advice, or intrusion, comes from a family member we like or respect, it's OK. If it comes from a peer we are not too fond of, we may take the suggestion because we know it's right, but inwardly resent the process. This happens every day. To make matters worse, we discover how easy it is to respond in kind to those who attempt to manipulate us.

As mentioned earlier, as a pastor, I devoted considerable

time to family counseling. I discovered that when problems develop between husband and wife, one person always seems to carry more hurt than the other, and usually the person bearing the most hurt is the one who tries to force behavioral change on the other. It never works! The partner who isn't hurting wants to have fun and get on with life. The one who is hurting wants to address problems, discuss faults, and convince the other of the need to change. This is never fun. Eventually the hurting party loses his or her ability to change the other, but keeps on trying, making things increasingly worse. The result is, while one hurts, the other finds someone to have fun with!

Good Things on the Job Happen to Happy People

Because attitude is a matter of choice, regardless of who is to blame, those suffering the hurt need to correct their attitude quickly or they will eventually destroy their chances of success and happiness in that particular ministry.

Be Happy—or Leave!

If you cannot be happy, the workplace holds little future for you, because in the workplace good things usually happen to happy people.

The apostle Paul said, "I have learned that in whatsoever state I am, therewith to be content." Paul discovered that, in situations he could not change, it was possible to have a good attitude and be content. If you know you are where God wants you to be, be happy! If you don't know this, consider a change.

Regardless of all the reasons why one becomes hurt, staying hurt is a matter of personal choice. People do themselves a disservice when they cloud up the workplace with unnecessary hurt and gloom, because good things on the job do happen to happy people! We all enjoy working with and taking direction from happy people

I recall hearing Dr. Tim Kimmel of Generation Ministries, lead a session on team building, using football as an example. Football, he said, is not a one-man situation—it requires team involvement to win. He mentioned that when a player fell on the field the coach would run up and ask, "Are you hurt or injured?" If the player replied "injured," the coach signaled for a stretcher to carry the player off the field. If the player said, "I'm hurt!" the coach would say, "get back in the game." Because the fastest way to get over hurts is to get back in the game and quit lying on the field. Once they are advancing up the field with their team, somehow those hurts seem to disappear!

It's the same in the Christian workplace. Hurt people need to get up, become active, and focus on the real enemy.

Your Happiness and Success Will Depend Primarily Upon Four Things:

1. Your ability to cope with a changing environment. (As Christians we can really do this!)
2. Your ability and willingness to adjust your expectations of others.(This we can also do!)
3. A willingness to take responsibility for your own decisions. This way you are less likely to ever feel used. (This one is a little harder.)
4. A commitment to protect family relationships. (This one calls for Grace!)

When Nehemiah was confronted by thousands of his workers, being a seasoned leader, he probably considered his options. Somehow I believe that if his team hadn't been involved in an extremely important project, he might have simply stood back and let the family members sort out their own problems. He took action because he believed in the eternal importance of what he and his workers were doing and the importance of who they were as God's family!

Because our situation is similar, we are responsible for doing whatever it takes to remove usury from our family workplace. We are God's family and our identity as such is at risk!

EIGHT

Nobody Wants to Feel "Used"

WHO HAS NOT FELT USED BY SOME FAMILY MEMBER? A GRANDmother said to me recently, "I love my grandchildren, but my daughter just uses me as a convenience. She takes it for granted that, without even asking, she can dump the kids off at grandma's! Don't get me wrong. I love my grandchildren, but I don't like being taken for granted. I feel used."

Visiting with a pastor several years ago, I listened as he described some of his plans for expanding various departments of his church. He did not have a large congregation, but seemed to be accomplishing an amazing amount of property development with those he had. During the conversation I said, "Pastor, it is obvious to me that your congregation understands the blessing to be enjoyed through giving. However, as an observer, it appears that some are giving of their time and money, almost to the point of neglecting their home responsibilities. Where does the money come from to care for all this expansion?"

He responded with a knowing smile.

"Don, I know my people. That's the key! You see, even though many are already giving sacrificially to various church projects, they always are willing to do more!"

I was still not satisfied, so I said, "I know you're an influential speaker, but how can you convince people who are already giving so much of their time and money to give sufficient to meet these enormous expansion plans?

"Don, with some in my congregation, all I need to do is mention their name in our church bulletin, or recognize them by name over the pulpit, and they'll do about anything I ask! You see, when you know these people as well as I do, you know what their "buttons" are."

This led to laughter and joking as various examples were given of the variety of buttons he could press that would cause individuals in his church to spring into action. One family would respond if requested by the pastor's wife, and a round of golf with the pastor would always result in cooperation from another. In each case it involved some special little touch from the pastor or his wife.

Still somewhat surprised by our conversation I jokingly said, "Somehow what you are describing seems like pure manipulation."

To which he replied, "No, it's merely a matter of me giving them what they want, which is recognition, and they giving me what I want—help on church projects."

In this particular example, who used whom the most? Or, was anybody used?

This is worth considering for a moment. The story reveals the temptations that come to each person in ministry, regardless of position. Our passion for ministry sometimes exceeds that of proclaiming the goodness of God's grace. We influence others, both in one-on-one conversation, and before assemblies of thousands. The greater our effectiveness in ministry, the greater our temptation to rely on our communication skills to accomplish various aspects of our goals. Similarly, I have sold thousands of dollars in advertising products because I knew what a client's "buttons" were. Workers and leaders alike are sometimes guilty of perfecting their ability to influence to the extent that it becomes manipulation. I call it misused trust. I'm not suggesting that each time a leader mentions a workers name in the church bulletin, that some ulterior motive exists. But sometimes? Taking advantage of another persons trust is a form of usury.

Before using powers of persuasion, leaders should first ask, "Am I doing this for them or for me?" "Trusting people" seldom suspect manipulation. However, we can be sure that somewhere down the road wrong motives will be discovered, and hurt and bitterness will result. It is possible for us to become so zealous in reaching our goals that we feel justified using nearly every creative method at our disposal.

Ministry Volunteers

It is obvious that God intends for the bulk of ministry work to be performed by volunteers. It has always been this way, and always will be.

God has given each person a unique combination of abilities, intended as gifts to the church. Each is blessed with the ability to minister God's love to others in ways unique to himself. Some excel in leadership, some as teachers, others in caring or serving, and some in administration. (Rom. 6:12 and 1 Cor. 12:4) Most ministries strive to nurture and cultivate these gifts through the guidance and accountability of the local church. To the degree that this is done, there is opportunity for fulfillment. To the degree that volunteers are guided into fields of service for which they are not qualified, it can be usury.

Volunteer ministry should be win-win! Volunteers should be fulfilled and the church properly served. They should recognize their gifts and make ministry decisions accordingly.

Every Person Involved In A Ministry Workplace Has Opportunity To Participate In The Practice Of Usury

- Christian leaders/employers/supervisors may solicit usury from their staffs.

- Christian staff members may also obtain usury from their leaders.
- Volunteers may have agendas that involve usury.
- Pastors may anticipate usury from volunteers and adherents.

For example, I am in a leadership or supervisory capacity. I am interviewing you for a staff position and, during the course of the interview, you mention that you are a Christian and have a genuine desire to use your talents in ministry. My expectations run exceptionally high. While you are answering my questions, I am thinking, "You could be exactly the person I am looking for. I can expect you to do or be the following."

1. You will have a high work ethic. ("You'll be great! The Bible contains an outstanding teaching on responsibility and stewardship.")
2. You will be honest. ("A quality rare in people today. Your religious convictions will produce honesty.")
3. You'll have a high standard of integrity. ("You impress me as the type of person who reads a chapter from *My Utmost for His Highest* every day. You will probably become so involved in the work of ministry that you'll never give a thought to when it's time to go home.")
4. You won't meddle in the affairs of others. ("As one committed to the teachings of the Bible, I'll be safe here.")
5. I know you'll be punctual. ("Being a Christian, you will not be slothful in your work.")
6. You'll respect your supervisors. ("You were no doubt taught to 'render unto Caesar the things that are Caesars.'")
7. You will be temperate in lifestyle. ("You have learned to be 'temperate in all things.'")
8. You seem polite and courteous. ("You have learned,

'be kind one to another' and 'in honor preferring one another' while in Sunday School.")

9. I believe you will be loyal. ("Your stated desire to be involved in ministry conveys a commitment to loyalty.")

And, a very special bonus!

10. Because of your expressed interest in ministry, you will undoubtedly accept a lower salary than I might have to pay someone else.

Now, before I make any observations, this is what you could be thinking.

"Won't it be wonderful working for a Christian boss! You will be . . ."

1. Kind and considerate. ("After some of the people I have worked for I finally have one who is a Christian. My last boss was frequently demanding and angry. This is going to be much different.")
2. Understanding. ("My last job was not part of the Christian workplace. I got written up every time I was a few minutes late. Somehow I expect you'll be a lot more understanding.")
3. Forgiving. ("I made quite a few mistakes on my last job, and my boss held it against me. Christians forgive and forget. Oh God, do let me get this job—I need a break!")
4. Sensitive to other's feelings. ("I'm a very sensitive person. My feelings get hurt easily. Here, I'll be safe!")
5. Patient. ("I'm rather a slow learner. I try hard, but it does take me a while to learn new things. You will be patient with me.")
6. Aware of my gifts in ministry. ("Because I'm a caring person, people will seek my counsel. You will be

pleased to have someone on staff who has a ministry like mine. I know I'll be given the opportunity to do some counseling.")

7. Understanding. ("As Christians we are family. At last I will have a boss who understands spiritual things and will want to see me attend various church retreats and conferences.")
8. Fair. ("There are so many places in Scripture that admonish Christian leaders to be generous and to reward those who work for them, such as 'a servant is worthy of his hire,' that I'll never have to ask for a raise. You'll do the right thing.")
9. A friend. ("In the event of emergency expenses, etc., I know you'll be there for me if I need you.")

In these examples, both employer and employee are already expecting more from the other than either can realistically deliver. No one can live up to the Christian expectations of another, which is why a workplace situation places relationships at risk. All parties are wise to break that ethereal spell and come down to reality.

Workplace Agendas

Sometimes workers have personal ministry agendas that exceed their job assignments. They seek a few personal benefits beyond those negotiated for. Recognizing this, each person should agree not to hold others responsible if some items on their unspoken wish list do not materialize.

The Myth of Ministry

When conducting a sales meeting at a Christian-formatted radio station, I asked a sales person,

"Did you have a good day yesterday?

To which she replied,

"I had a wonderful day!"

Expecting to hear a glowing report of some excellent selling, I went on,

> "Please tell me about it. How much did you sell?"
>
> "Oh, Mr. Cartmell, I didn't sell anything! Yesterday turned out to be my day for ministry! God had a wonderful day planned for me."

Somewhat puzzled I continued,

> "Are you saying that you didn't make any sales calls all day?"
>
> "That's right, I had intended to, but starting with my first call, I just knew God had other plans for the day. I really didn't even try to sell. This was my day for ministry!"
>
> "Did you forget that you are being paid to sell? We have an entire staff dependent upon the sales your department makes. If you have a personal desire to minister, you could have done so during your lunch or coffee breaks."
>
> "Well, knowing this to be a Christian company, I just figured that you'd understand and be pleased."

A few years later I had a conversation with a radio announcer.

> "Bruce, I need to talk with you a few minutes about your air shift."
>
> "Fine, Mr. Cartmell."

> "I would like you to tighten up your announcing segments between selections. They are becoming too long."
>
> "But, Mr. Cartmell, those times are very important to me. That is when I do my personal ministry!"
>
> "I appreciate your desire to minister, but with the trend your program is taking you'll soon have more talking than music. We must let the music do the bulk of the ministering. God has inspired songwriters with some extremely effective lyrics."
>
> "Mr. Cartmell, I hear what you are saying, but I really can't do what you are asking, because, the way I see it, when the song is playing I'm working for you, but when my mike is open, I'm working for God. I just thought, this being a Christian company, you would want it this way."

It is interesting that each employee expressed sentiments to the effect that "I thought this was a Christian company." Each *used* the company to satisfy his own personal agendas. One had been hired to sell advertising, the other to do a tight air shift. Each expected more from the company than was reasonable.

The above situations are cases involving stewardship. Each person applied for and accepted a position with a Christian company. They each knew and understood what was expected of them and for several months were exemplary workers. However, eventually it became evident that their own agendas for ministry took precedence over the needs of the employer. They both resisted direction in this regard.

Using Church as a Client Base for Business Can Involve Usury

Is it conceivable that those who volunteer their services to a church or other organization might also have a personal business agenda?

I was in discussion with the pastor of a large metropolitan church. He mentioned that about fifteen hundred people in his congregation were active in ministry within his church.

"Pastor, I'm missing something here. You have a church of about four thousand members and a pastoral staff of fifteen hundred? What am I missing?"

"Don't get me wrong, Don. I'm the senior pastor, but my church has grown to the size that I am able to do little more than be the Sunday pulpit speaker and care for church administration. I find it necessary to delegate the greater percentage of pastoral care to volunteers in my congregation."

He then described the large base of volunteers who lead home groups, singles groups, senior citizen groups, and so forth, in addition to those who assist in Sunday school and the music department.

Perhaps it was just my suspicious mind, but while he was describing the structure of his church, I said to myself, "I can only imagine the tons of multi-level products that flow through this congregation." Is it possible that some of these volunteers in ministry might expect usury from others, as an added agenda? Think of how many people across America have accepted volunteer ministry positions in their churches with the additional business agenda of using church members as a core for their network marketing, insurance sales, or health products business. Naturally, Christians will do business with other Christians, in and out of church, and they should. But whenever family members are placed in a position of unreasonable obligation, it becomes usury. People don't attend a worship service so they can be subjected to one's personal marketing plan. It can place a strain on relationships.

Social Workplace Agendas

In the general market, people seek employment as a stepping stone along their career path. Their social life is usually centered outside the workplace. However, in the ministry workplace, things are different because it's family. It is not unusual for one to enter the Christian workplace seeking social fulfillment.

People don't attend a worship service so they can be subjected to one's personal marketing plan.

"I think it will be wonderful working with Christians. Finding new Christian friends has always been difficult for me. This position is just what I've needed."

When I was a teenager, I felt a strong spiritual pull to sing in the church choir. Many adults in our church appreciated my commitment to ministry. Their precious Donnie really had a heart for God. What they didn't know was that my main reason for being there was a couple of sharp-looking ladies in the alto section. I discovered that I wasn't the only one with this secret agenda in our choir. In fact, there were times when our choir performed better socially than vocally.

Sometimes there is the declared reason for what we do in ministry and also the more complete reason. Any agenda that imposes unnecessary stress on another member of family could easily become usury. Because we each desire personal fulfillment, it is natural for us to seek lasting relationships within the workplace. The key to much of this chapter is, "Don't press!" Try to respect the right of each worker to seek fulfillment, remembering that our particular agendas may, or may not be the answer to their needs.

A workplace proverb might be in order, even though I realize no one will heed it:

"Do thy best not to fall in love with someone in thine own office or workplace. Thou canst create many unfortunate problems for thyself and others, especially if thine heart later becomes broken."

Usury Didn't Start in the '60s

Jesus gathered some volunteers around Him. He referred to them as His disciples. Would it be conceivable that some of them had secret agendas? It was only natural for some to consider, "If Jesus is going to be establishing His own Kingdom, I run a good chance of being part of His cabinet if I get on the inside track now." It makes sense. The only "kingdoms" they could relate to involved rulership and control. Jesus certainly had the charisma and ability needed to attract and satisfy crowds. He could achieve Kingdom rule. This could be their chance!

The teachings and miracles of Jesus impressed the disciples. Being a disciple provided an opportunity to develop a close relationship with *One who spoke and did things unlike any other!* They were fascinated by His miracles. An invitation to follow Jesus was intriguing. Perhaps He would impart to them the ability also to perform miracles! Some of these agendas became obvious during the few years they were together. But, *knowing the thoughts and intents of their hearts*, Jesus helped them restore proper focus. He took them to Gethsemene, and on to Calvary. He still does. A visit to Calvary has a wonderful way of helping present-day disciples assess their true motives.

A few had agendas that went beyond discipleship. Two wanted assurances that they would have key positions in heaven. Jesus made it clear that there was no merit in trying to lobby for positions in the Kingdom of God. Nor should there be value in lobbying in the Christian workplace today. Therefore, if we have any workplace agendas that are either manipulative or unethical toward those we associate with, we should let them go! If we have secret agendas or ambitions that relate to careers or social networking, let us make a sincere commitment that we will not hold others responsible if these agendas are not satisfied.

If we have secret agendas that could affect our attitude if not satisfied, we should discuss these with the person we would hold responsible, before accepting a workplace assignment.

NINE

Tomorrow and Beyond

It matters not how many brothers or sisters you have, nor how different your goals and careers may be. We all have one thing in common: we are growing older each day and moving steadily toward our senior years at exactly the same speed. Each member of your family will reach their retirement years in a different state of preparedness, depending largely upon decisions made earlier. For those in the Christian workplace, decisions made along the way make all the difference.

As mentioned in Chapter 6, involvement in ministry work spans an economic spectrum from those who volunteer in ministry, to others who have prepared for their calling, and look to ministry to provide financial necessities for their families. In business, some too consider their work as a calling, and have combined ministry with a business career. Each is part of the Christian workplace.

I do not suggest that those who sacrifice the most financially are necessarily more committed to ministry than others. God has a plan for every life. Each person is responsible to Him to honestly assess their God given abilities in ministry, and make their personal, family, career, financial and ministry-calling decisions accordingly.

Ministry in America Is Changing!

Today, most who earn the right to lead in pastoral, counseling, or other types of ministry invest years in college or university, preparing for service at significant cost. Large metro areas require knowledgeable and capable communicators as pastors. "Mega" churches are built to accommodate thousands, at a cost of millions, in total contrast to my earlier years. I recall how our pastor and his family occupied an apartment at the rear of the church and received an offering of $35 a week. Not much, but people gave them vegetables, roasts, pies, and so forth, to help. Things have changed in America, but pastoral life in many parts of the world continues much as I have described.

It is easy to be consumed by the satisfying and rewarding elements of ministry to the extent that one feels guilty considering financial matters.

God still calls His people into various forms of ministry and service, sometimes at great sacrifice, and other times, inspired by this same Christian message, people respond to a calling that allows them to blend business careers with ministry. Today, a sizable Christian consumer base also exists for Christian books, music, entertainment products, and media services, and thousands have responded to satisfy this need. Fortunately, even though the ministry/business world has become somewhat complex, the Christian message penetrates the nations of the world to an unprecedented degree. Every technological development in communication is being used to spread the Gospel.

Consider the thousands of pockets of Christians who work side by side in their chosen business, church ministry, or related Christian organization. They exist to the degree that God blesses the vision and efforts of the leaders and the many people who work by their side.

Those employed in ministry or Christian-type organizations or businesses progress slowly along the road toward eventual retirement. Along this road it is easy to be consumed by the satisfying and rewarding elements of ministry to the extent that one feels guilty considering financial matters. As a result, many important financial decisions that should be dealt with today, are put off till tomorrow.

I remember hearing a Bible teacher describe the fright that can enter a man's heart when he realizes that age has crept along faster than he realized, and that there is no longer time to accomplish all the things he had planned. When we are young, we seldom give old age a thought. To the young there will always be time to care for retirement issues. We should consider the fact that, even though America is a land of opportunity, an alarming percentage of adults are nearing their golden years unprepared. This is true in the general marketplace, but, because of the complexity of ministry today, it is an even greater reality among Christians in ministry work. Here, young and middle-aged Christians frequently assume that, because they are involved in ministry, somehow things will be OK. Millions are the stories told by those who gave their lives in the work of ministry but failed to make adequate provision for their later years.

I have made frequent reference to the fact that unrealistic expectations cause considerable stress within ministries. Financial expectations within the Christian workplace sometimes intensify when people get older. Having invested many years in ministry, some unrealistically look to others to compensate for their lack of preparation. These unrealistic expectations place relationships at risk.

I believe it is essential for those in Christian work to carefully consider what prompted them to enter some aspect of ministry. Was it a calling? Or, were they simply in need of a job, and thought it could be a good change working alongside other

Christians? An honest answer can be a valuable basis for future financial or career decisions. We should also recognize that the work of ministry will continue whether or not we happen to be filling a particular role.

Up until now our focus has been on addressing workplace issues that contribute to relational stress between workers in ministry. This chapter does too, but also expresses concern for the personal welfare of workers and their families. To those who view their work in ministry as their life's commitment or calling, what about tomorrow—and beyond?

We arrive at an important question: What approach should those in Christian work take in regard to the retirement issue?

It is obviously not the responsibility of church organizations or businesses to automatically guarantee comfortable sailing for each worker throughout their retirement years. This would not only break the financial back of any business or ministry, but would also encourage people to avoid making responsible decisions. Instead, the responsibility rests with each individual to make decisions that will help them meet personal objectives. It is extremely easy for workers to become trapped between the pull of ministry and their financial responsibilities to family. A very fine line exists between the faith walk and the ministry career walk, because both involve ministry. Few families in ministry have not experienced these tensions. Having said that, I also believe Christian organizations or businesses that serve some aspect of ministry have unique family responsibilities that, in many cases, could reduce worker stress related to this issue.

God's Provision for His Family, Years Ago!

Two Old Testament entrepreneurs provide us with examples of a "caring" concept, initiated by God for His family.

The book of Samuel, in the Old Testament, records the exciting episodes in King David's life. David was a true entrepreneur.

Courage to conquer! Vision! Energy! He also had an amazingly simple faith and trust in God.

There was an underlying element in David's relationship with God, and with the children of Israel, that contributed to his success.

We read, "And David knew that the Lord had established him as king over Israel and had exalted his kingdom for the sake of His people Israel." (2 Sam 4:12)

Later, Solomon enjoyed phenomenal success as King of Israel. Interestingly, he also perpetuated this philosophy of caring for God's family to the degree that it became obvious to outsiders.

When the Queen of Sheba visited Solomon, even though an outsider, she stood amazed at how God had blessed Israel. She said to King Solomon, "How happy your men must be! How happy your officials who continually stand before you and hear your wisdom! Praise be to the Lord your God, who has delighted in you and placed you on the throne of Israel. Because of the Lord's eternal love for Israel, he has made you king, to maintain justice and righteousness." (1 Kings 10:8-9)

These two kings held to the understanding that the prime reason they were anointed by God and granted success as rulers was due to God's great love for Israel!

God Expects Members of His Family to Be Supervised in Righteousness

We are safe to draw some conclusions from these two great rulers of Israel because of their significance. David is described as being a man after God's own heart, and Scripture credits Solomon as being the wisest man that ever lived. These two divinely appointed leaders had gained insights into the heart of God. They understood that God desires members of His family to be cared for in righteousness and justice! His people were not to be used nor taken advantage of.

God had placed David and Solomon in their respective positions of leadership to implement His purposes. God uniquely blessed David and Solomon as gifted leaders. He gave them exceptional entrepreneurial gifts, spiritual insights, wisdom, and courage. They were humble enough to understand that the victories in battle, and the acquired wealth of Israel, were blessings from God that occurred because of His love for His Family. This has never changed!

God had many reasons for wanting to bless Israel. He wanted other nations to observe His righteousness. He desired people around the world to acknowledge the fact that the God of Israel was the only true God and that He had a loving and caring relationship with His people.

Today, most Christian organizations have their own mission statements. These could include the proclaiming of the Gospel, providing Biblical teaching for the edification of believers, evangelism, international outreach, meeting special needs of the inner city, compassion, and so on. My observations are that, regardless how carefully our mission statements are framed, God's plans will always exceed our own creativity.

A few years ago I encouraged a talented broadcaster to become the host of a talk show. He agreed. During the next few years his success caused his show to expand to several markets across the nation. I didn't know that in one of the cities we added to his network lived a close relative that he hadn't seen for over thirty-five years. He had no idea where she was or even if she was still alive. One day she and her husband were driving along, listening to a Christian radio show in one of these many cities. They *happened* to be listening to this particular syndicated talk show.

The name was right, but could it really be him? Could he really be a Christian?

Within hours these two were reconnected, after all these years! We had our programming and business reasons for developing that network of stations, but God had some additional reasons that we knew nothing about. This is always the case.

Is it stretching things to believe that God has similarly blessed your ministry or workplace with gifted leaders who possess vision, charisma, wisdom, and courage, and that He intends that those within your ministry be cared for in righteousness and justice? Something to consider.

There are a million ways that love, care, and righteousness can be expressed. Suffice it to say that whatever form it takes should be a testimony to the identity that God intends for His family.

The CEO of an extremely fast growing and successful telecommunications company says,

"I may be a number cruncher, but I don't think it's a coincidence that a company that really found its heart is this successful. This company's success is inextricably tied to the happiness of our employees."

This company, which developed one of the most attractive employee benefit packages in the country, makes no claims about being part of the Christian workplace, but where do you think the CEO picked up the principle of caring and righteousness—that it's *"better to give than to receive"*?

Without question, the Christian workplace should exemplify the righteousness of God. However, if yours doesn't, here are a few ways you can protect the welfare of your own family.

1. If one does not have sufficient financial resources to provide for present and future needs, he or she should probably pass up an opportunity to invest prime years in a ministry or workplace that offers only minimal salary and benefits. That is, unless specifically called by God to do so.
2. When people accept positions in the Christian workplace, believing they are where God wants them to be, they should accept the terms they negotiate and be happy. If those arrangements later prove inadequate, they should consider leaving.

3. Take full responsibility for your own decisions. To trust that everything will work out, just because it is ministry, is not realistic.
4. Insist on an honest relationship between you and your leader. Address any vague or possibly misleading statements that need to be clarified, such as, "If you really help this organization grow you'll be rewarded in a big way!" Ambiguous statements like this can be misleading.
5. When considering the Christian workplace as an ongoing part of your career or calling, you are wise to do your own careful investigation. That way, you can discover whether or not a genuine program of caring is in place, which will provide you with important information upon which to base your decisions.

Investigate Before Joining

Talk with some people already on the job. Listen to what is said and what is not said. Try to sense the atmosphere of the workplace. Ask questions like, "People don't look too happy here—what's going on?" Or, "Why is everyone so happy: is it always this way?" Or, "If you could change one thing about this organization what would it be?" Questions that can be answered "yes" or "no" are of little value.

Obtain the names of people who recently left the organization. Ask them questions like, "I'm considering taking a position with your previous company. Tell me, why did it not become a career place for you?" Ask these same questions of two or three previous workers and see if a pattern emerges.

If a negative pattern emerges, don't say, "It will be different with me." It won't. In some ways those at the top of an organization are no different from the rest of us. They are not inclined to change what seems to be working. We don't—they don't.

Don't risk being another statistic, even if it means not accepting the type of ministry position you desire.

When righteousness prevails, things always seem to work better. They say in the accommodation business that hotels lose towels only to the extent that guests feel they have been overcharged. The workplace is similar. When Sermon on the Mount principles are practiced within the workplace, attitudes and efficiency improve. A dynamic of caring should be evident in every ministry and Christian business or organization, so that "outsiders," like the Queen of Sheba of old, will recognize a work environment where righteousness and justice prevails.

Like the mechanic who is so busy helping fix other people's cars that he never takes time to fix his own, many in ministry do the same. We become immersed with the warmth and excitement that comes by helping people learn to trust Jesus. We'll take time to counsel them about their walk with God, their family matters, and financial stewardship, but frequently fail to provide the same degree of concern for our own families.

Today you may be young and feel as though you have all the time in the world to become responsible and make important long-term financial decisions. Or perhaps you're middle-aged and enjoying your ministry work intensely. Jesus taught us not to *worry* about tomorrow. Worry gets us nowhere. Instead, I encourage you to be mindful of the times, ever-conscious of the fact that we each are moving slowly, but steadily, toward those senior years. Wise decisions today can protect some valuable Christian relationships tomorrow.

May you have no regrets.

TEN

Me, Work for My Brother or Sister?

I REMEMBER AN OCCASION WHEN I WAS ASKED TO BABY SIT A couple of youngsters. I watched as the elder brother tried to oversee the activities of the younger. Finally, feeling smothered and frustrated by the continuous flow of orders from his brother, the youngest shouted, "I don't have to take orders from you. You're not my mom or dad!"

To the degree that we acknowledge the dynamics of family in the Christian workplace, we understand the necessity for great wisdom in our supervisory decisions. If God is our Heavenly Father, and we are His children, then in His eyes we are about as much family as it gets. It is therefore logical for us to study relationships between family members engaged in a typical family enterprise, to help us understand the opportunities and challenges found within the Christian workplace.

One seldom elects to work either for family, with family, or have family work for them, because they value family relationships above any business advantage that might occur from the blending of family resources or energies. Whenever family members choose to do otherwise, they usually will first become satisfied that the advantages or obligations upon them as family are sufficient to justify the risks involved in blending family and business.

There are risks.

Family businesses normally run quite smoothly as long as father or mother is at the helm. When the going is a little rough, the children can at least assume the organization they are helping to build will one day be theirs. Of additional advantage is the fact that brothers and sisters have grown up accustomed to parental guidance and authority. It is therefore usually easier for siblings to accept direction from a parent than from a brother or sister.

If God is our Heavenly Father, and we are His children, then we are as much family as it gets.

When the siblings eventually have a turn at the controls, the risk of relational problems increases. They are subjected to the temptations of sibling rivalry. To add to the complexity of the situation, each spouse also helps determine the quality of relationships.

Joys and Sorrows of a Family Business

In every family business there are bound to be some absolutely great times, as well as some periods of relational tension. Solutions to relational stresses are usually more complex in a family environment. As we have already discussed, within family the resolution of tensions usually takes a while. If relational problems become intense, it is not unusual for a sibling to feel confined to a family prison. Siblings are forced to wrestle with the prospect that if they leave the business, they lose their chances to gain financially from the business, and, if they stay, they are faced with the prospect of continued emotional stress and tension. If they leave, due to family tension, relational risks increase. Family embarrassment or financial hardship may result from such a move. The option is to stay, but by doing so, family members can feel sentenced to a relational prison that seems harder to escape from than walls topped with barbed wire.

Sometimes family obligations mandate that siblings participate in a family enterprise. Frequently they are faced with responsibilities that only family can assume,which is somewhat similar to the Christian workplace!

It isn't that Christians want to work with each other, as much as the fact that there is a job to be done that family members must do! Jesus challenged His disciples with the responsibility of infiltrating the world with the "good news of the Gospel of Christ." As family members, we accept the challenge but in doing so also acknowledge the relational risks.

There is too much at stake to do otherwise. In spite of these risks, ministries and Christian businesses have been developed throughout the world. In each situation, members of God's family participate together in Kingdom business. Their effectiveness is always in direct proportion to their family relationships. That's why the removal of usury is essential. Eliminate usury, and workplace problems nearly take care of themselves.

We should acknowledge three things:

1. The Christian workplace is a family situation. Relationships are delicate and require special care.
2. Usury must be addressed. The admonitions in Scripture to *love one another* and *in honor preferring one another* exist as essential formulas to protect these relationships.
3. Within the Christian workplace some brothers and sisters will achieve positions of visibility, power, and affluence, while others will fill important but less visi-

> ble roles. It is essential that siblings be completely honest with themselves in regard to their personal gifts and abilities. They need to know who they are and what they do best. Whenever possible, siblings should be active in roles appropriate to their special abilities.

TV infomercials tell us that "you can do and be whatever you want and decide to be!" To some degree, this is true. We can always be stretched beyond where we are today. But when you add the words "happy, satisfied and content" to this phrase, it becomes false. Scripture explains that we are made like the various parts of a body. Each has special and discrete gifts and abilities. When people are misplaced in their roles, usury always results. The principle contributing factor is family!

I'll Never Work for My Brother/Sister!

In the Christian workplace you undoubtedly will! So let's see how we can make this work.

During the early years of my career, when I was in my early twenties, I was personnel officer in a large military garrison—responsible for the employment of about four hundred people. I took some needed training in management, during which I learned an important key to worker success and worker fulfillment.

1. Make yourself indispensable.
2. Make yourself dispensable.

Due to the family dynamic, these two steps are extremely important within ministries. With an abundance of siblings present in a workplace, it is important not only that supervisors perform their responsibilities, but they must be perceived by staff as being suitable and qualified for their positions. These two steps accomplish this.

Make Yourself Indispensable!

Step 1 says make a commitment to do such a great job that you will become recognized as indispensable by staff and supervisors alike.

This requires that you focus on that position, content in the knowledge that you know you are where you are intended to be. Stay there until no one can dispute your competency in that role. This process helps you avoid sibling suspicion that you are attempting to "politic" your way to the top, a practice that never works well in a ministry. Commit to doing your job better than anyone else has done.

Make Yourself *Dispensable!*

Step 2 says feel sufficiently secure in your position that you will willingly mentor someone else in your role, without having any plans or knowledge of a better position to promote to. This requires that you find someone to mentor, with the risk that they may learn how to do your job even better than you do it. This is the sign of a real leader!

Many times, capable people miss promotions only because there is no one ready to take their place when the opportunity arrives. One can rarely anticipate when someone is going to leave an organization or business, or when expansion is going to create a promotional opportunity. All too frequently, a replacement is needed now! The person who makes him or herself dispensable is ready to promote at a moment's notice.

Promotions Within a Family Business

Who wouldn't be delighted to receive a promotion? Within a family business promotions should be addressed with great care. Christians tend to be sensitive people. They have been touched by Calvary's love, resulting in increased sensitivities to the needs of others, but also to their own desires and feelings.

When someone in a family workplace receives a promotion, some family member will undoubtedly ask, "Why her?" "Why him?"

Wise employers and supervisors eliminate much of this potential for stress and perceived usury by making staff choices that are easily recognized by the workers as being wise. People seeking promotions should *run the race to win,* but also strive to be recognized by others as being worthy of the promotions they accept. Such people will usually receive the peer support needed for success.

It's one thing to get a promotion, and another to be supported by those needed to make your programs work. In one sense, expecting workers in ministry to support a supervisor unqualified for a position is a form of usury. It requires family members to give that which is unreasonable.

In regard to working for a sibling, almost everyone does it during a career in ministry. There are risks and there are challenges, but this is a family situation and, for the sake of family, we can make it work—that is, when we don't expect more from others than what is reasonable.

ELEVEN

How to Supervise Family

PARENTS TEND TO BECOME AMATEUR PSYCHOLOGISTS AS THEY attempt to guide the growth and development of each child. Each child has a different personality. The major challenge in parenting is to help each child respond to the guidance of love. Parents learn the necessity of using different techniques with each child. The Christian workplace is similar.

In short, we should be caring, sensitive, happy, positive, honest, and firm!

Every Christian workplace comprises ministry and business. An even greater challenge exists for some in leadership—that of determining how much Christianity to infuse into their management style. The love of God will enhance one's personality and character and add a marvelous dynamic to one's leadership style, if given a chance. Christians who try to appear all business by filtering out the compassionate attributes of God's love create workplace confusion.

Some never really get a handle on combining supervision with their Christian faith. They appear as one thing to the public and another to those with whom they work. They can be warm, caring, spiritual, and even pastoral, but if they sense that a worker has a personal request—flip—they immediately switch to a hard-nosed, impersonal business person. If it weren't so sad, it would be humorous watching them flip through their different personas, as though they were surfing channels on TV.

One situation will describe what I mean. A number of years ago Nikki, my wife,and I were house-hunting. One day, while scouting a pleasant neighborhood, we spotted a "for sale by owner" sign. We knocked, and a very agreeable lady invited us in. During our visit we learned that this lady and her husband pastored a fairly large church in the area. A few weeks later we met the pastor and enjoyed our conversation together. They were great people! As for the house, there was nothing wrong with it if you liked blue and didn't mind traffic noise. We liked these people and desired to know them better. Even though the house was not everything we were looking for, we decided to give at least some thought as to how we could make it feel like home. We swallowed hard when we learned their asking price, because it was outrageous.

Later they called and invited us to breakfast. Breakfast was another pleasant experience—well, up to a point. About midway through the meal, I mentioned that we had determined to purchase within our means. I said that, although the house could possibly suit our needs, we would not be able to pay more than a certain amount. I told them that their friendship was of greater value to us than their house and that we were not about to ask them to lower their price for us. The pastor's countenance changed, and he bristled with anger. The atmosphere of our breakfast conversation turned icy cold. The pastor's wife blushed in embarrassment and looked down at her plate. Breakfast ended with little more than small talk.

Even though he had preached dozens of messages extolling the merits of family stewardship, it seemed to irritate him to have invited us to breakfast if it was not going to result in the sale of his house.

Skillful at developing new relationships, he continues to

pastor a large church. But with all of his learning he has not discovered how to radiate Christ when business isn't going his way. He flipped his attitude channels until he found one to suit the business occasion—and lost a friend.

To those who struggle with their workplace identity, please leave the struggle behind and radiate Christ in all that you do! All the attributes needed in leadership, management or supervision are found in Christ. Caring, sensitivity, happiness, attitude, honesty and firmness, can all be beautifully blended together into one magnificent leader, whether in ministry or business!

These characteristics are important in any supervisory role, but are specially needed when supervising family.

Supervise by Caring

How I wish supervisors would realize that there is nothing risky or weak about caring. The same methods Jesus used in leading and mentoring His disciples will work in any contemporary management or supervisory role. We, who are the beneficiaries of His love, seem reluctant to pass along these same blessings to others. The ideal Christian leader allows the love of God to flow through his or her personality and talents. If the leader is not comfortable allowing Christ to be visible in all that he or she does, why build a career or business around the concept of Calvary?

Caring leadership is neither soft nor hard. "Caring" doesn't mean the leader is an administrative pushover. It ensures that supervisory relationships are built on a platform of respect and understanding. This is never wrong!

The Bible has great balance when it comes to supervisory authority. Throughout the Old Testament and New, we are given counsel and promises relating to stewardship and assurances of blessing to the diligent, with equal admonition to give justice to the dishonest and slothful.

I'm convinced that it's healthy for your staff to see you when you are upset, irritated, or even angry, if shortly thereafter they also see you when you are touched, grieved, and sorrowful over something. It's also important to be seen happy and excited. A Christian supervisor should be all of these things. Christian leadership is balance! Caring is an essential part of that balance.

Years ago it was necessary for me to terminate an employee who had been with me for about four years. I had invested much time and effort helping him to succeed, but his own agenda got in the way of success and it was time for a change.

I'll never forget that occasion. I visited him at his office one morning, and gently but firmly broke the news. We talked about his personal goals, his performance, and where he had failed to respond to our coaching. We talked as he cleaned out his desk, removed his family pictures from the walls, and placed his personal items in a box. When he was finished and it was time to leave, he came over to me, hugged me, and said, "Don, I just want to thank you for everything you've done, and for the sensitive manner in which you have dealt with me today."

Supervisory resources for Christians are vast. There is grace and wisdom available from God for every employee situation.

Supervise with Sensitivity

Be sensitive to the needs and feelings of others. When supervising family, if firmness is coupled with sensitivity, you'll be amazed by the positive results. Family always expects family to be sensitive, and why not?

Everyone's feelings are important! There will never be a situation when being sensitive to another person's feelings is wrong or ineffective. It never impedes a supervisor's ability to manage. I don't know how many times I have tried to understand the demeaning, insensitive approach used by some. It seems that in their calculating minds they say to themselves, "I need to tell Harry exactly what I think, but if I can wait until he is standing with a group of his peers, I'll be able to send the same message to each of them at the same time."

Sensitivity acknowledges that the feelings of the person supervised are of equal importance to those of the supervisor. There is something very Christian about conveying this understanding.

Supervise with Happiness

A happy workplace averts more family problems than we will ever know! Happiness is a major part of our relationship immune system. Whenever supervisors create an atmosphere of happiness, rather than fear and intimidation, there is less turnover in staff, and worker complaints nearly disappear. People just don't want to leave a happy place.

A family where laughter is seldom present is a family where stress is always present!

Happiness should flow from the top. The Bible provides numerous illustrations that indicate the need for authority, inspiration, and motivation to flow from the top to everyone in the workplace. Supervisory attitudes and priorities ripple down through the ranks, flavoring each level of supervision within an organization. These can be ripples of fear, intimidation, frustration, or uncertainty, but they can also be ripples of happiness, peace, and assurance. These have a tremendous affect on the productivity of a workplace. Happiness can always be introduced into the workplace by you, regardless of where you are on the organizational chart. It surely helps when it flows from the top, but this is one of the challenges we expressed earlier. Too many visionaries use their energy to make people happy on the outside and tend to forget the needs of those on the inside. People need to have fun at work. Sometimes the work of ministry becomes heavy. Workers become exposed to so many problems and needs that an outburst of laughter can be therapeutic. The workplace should be a place where people work hard—and laugh just as hard. A family where laughter is seldom present is a family where stress is always present.

If leaders provide an atmosphere that is not intimidating nor threatening, they create a natural environment for happiness. People want to be happy. A workplace will be happy if management simply provides the correct environment. The best part is, it doesn't cost a penny to produce.

Supervise with a Positive Attitude

Much of the stress and friction that occur between family members can be neutralized when exposed to a supervisor's positive attitude. Allow workplace attitudes to turn negative, and within days worker morale drops and tensions rise.

Positive attitudes do not just happen. They are the result of a person's choice.

There have been times when I returned home after an emotionally taxing day and began sharing my blues with Nikki. Her typical response is, "Stop, I don't want to hear this. We don't have any room for negative people in this house!" Filled with shame, I ceased my complaining, and discovered once again that attitude is an optional thing. It's our choice. A supervisor's role is to create a work environment conducive to good attitudes. For starters they can ask themselves, "Am I treating my people fairly?" "Does my method of delegation convey trust? " "Do I compliment and encourage sufficiently?"

Four hours a day of motivational hype will not correct workplace attitudes with workers who feel used financially or otherwise. Thousands of supervisors and workers in ministry are struggling with their attitudes because they have not been delegated sufficient authority with which to perform their responsibilities. Remember, this is family, and if family members are not provided with adequate authority to fulfill responsibilities, they'll be sure to wonder why. Family members are typically quick to draw their own conclusions.

Not all employee benefits cost money! In fact, some of the most important ones cost nothing. A troubled workplace can sometimes be fixed with a simple "thank you."

I hate to lay another "when I was a boy" story on you, but this should help make the point.

I mentioned earlier that at home on our hillside farm we used our team to yard timber out of the back section of our property. I commented about the crooked trail, engineered by the cows, that led to the back section.

I want to talk about our cows.

During my teenage years, one of my after-school chores was to walk up into the back section, find the cows, and bring them down to the barn for milking. In spring and summer they loved to wander through the woods and eat the tender leaves and shrubs.

One at a time I would guide the cows to the pathway. When I had them all together, I'd give them a shout of encouragement to get them moving in single formation down the hillside. Once moving, we were fine. I'd bring up the rear and give them repeated shouts so that they'd know I was there. As long as I kept to this routine, all was well.

As a typical teenager, I was easily distracted. About halfway down the hill I would often spot a bird or some animal tracks that I didn't recognize. I'd stop to investigate. The absence of my encouraging shouts from the rear became a signal to the cows that I no longer cared what they did, and within seconds they would disperse in all directions and resume eating leaves. When my personal explorations were finished and I returned to the path, the cows would be missing, and I'd have to start the process all over again.

Now, the way to supervise family is not to come behind

shouting—in fact, that's the worst way (although it worked for the cows). In case you missed it, the moral of this story is this: if you don't keep your team moving and motivated, their minds will wander and you'll waste a lot of time. Words of encouragement are wonderful motivators!

Supervise with Honesty

Does it seem unusual that I would mention honesty as an essential supervisory tool in the Christian workplace? We should perhaps take this one for granted.

I'm going to assume that all leaders in ministry consider honesty as a high personal priority. I want to discuss some dishonesty that is rather borderline (if there is such a thing).

When a worker asks, "I want to be earning $50,000 within two years. Can it happen on this job?"

A borderline honest answer would be, "Well, no one has ever made that amount in your position before, but who knows? Maybe you'll be the first. It could happen, if you do an outstanding job!"

Dishonest only in part. The supervisor never promised to pay that amount, nor did she provide a formula for doing so but, wanting to please, encouraged the worker to believe it could happen if he does an outstanding job. If a supervisor has no intention of paying the amount named, an honest answer would go something like this: "No, I doubt that you could ever receive what you desire in this particular position. It just doesn't pay that much. Perhaps this job isn't for you on a long-term basis. Your best chance to make that amount would be to eventually promote to something that pays a higher salary. This, of course, would depend upon a position becoming available for which you are qualified."

Honest answers eliminate usury. They create trust in the workplace. Remember that you are dealing with family. When too much is left to the other person's imagination, the possibility of perceived usury increases.

Many years ago, in a personnel capacity, I reviewed dozens of employee files, seeking information relating to worker problems. On numerous occasions I found nothing in the files relating to the complaints. I had been advised previously by various supervisors that many worker-problems existed, but found very little to substantiate these claims. I eventually discovered that some supervisors, not wanting to demotivate workers, avoided one-on-one discussions with them because that would have necessitated a report. This was a form of dishonesty. These employees were given the impression that all was well, when in fact many of them were on the verge of losing their jobs.

Loving Confrontation

In the Christian workplace supervisors are typically reluctant to be straight-forward when dealing with worker situations. Family members tend to avoid family confrontation, which—while understandable—is borderline dishonesty. Loving confrontation is not something to be feared. The results can be gratifying.

There is a simple, three-step preparation I follow before engaging in difficult or delicate worker discussions.

1. I search my heart for motives.
    - "Do I have a desire to give vent to my frustrations?"
    - "Do I desire to get even with this individual for all the trouble he or she has caused?"
    - "Can I truthfully say that what I intend to address is for the benefit of the other person, as well as for the organization?"
    - "Can I conduct this meeting with love and caring?"
    - "Will the meeting be void of attempt to intimidate or manipulate?"

2. Make sure I have my facts straight.
    - "This meeting could affect the career of another family member. Have I done adequate research in

preparation for the meeting?"
- "Have I given careful thought as to the implications of what I plan to discuss? Where could this discussion lead?"

3. I am prepared to live with the results.
    - There are no guarantees when dealing with sensitive worker challenges. We can seldom predict accurately what the other person's reaction or response will be. Therefore, do I sufficiently believe in the correctness of my position that I will be content to deal with the fallout?
    - When I feel comfortable on these three counts, I move forward.

Supervise with Firmness

Good workplace relationships depend on an element of structure. Firm boundary lines must exist. Employees should experience the safety and dependability of established boundaries. Firmness, without these other five leadership elements will stir up resentment and distrust. Add firmness to the other five, and supervisory firmness will generate confidence. Without firmness workers tend to feel insecure and unsupervised. Add the other five elements and workers feel safe.

I haven't added wisdom as a seventh leadership requirement because, I reasoned, if supervisors focus on caring, sensitivity, happiness, a positive attitude, honesty, and firmness, it is obvious they're doing something right!

Perhaps you are not involved in a specific leadership or supervisory role. This chapter is of importance to you in that leadership has a significant bearing upon all ministry relationships. Everyone in the workplace, regardless of position, should understand and appreciate the essential ingredients in effective leadership, management, and supervision, because a Christian workplace lacking these essentials will present some unnecessary relationship challenges.

Finally, let's say that your resume reflects that you have about thirty years in successful management experience. Please recognize that managing a family business or organization is different. Managing a ministry workplace is even more different! The expectation of trust in the Christian workplace calls for a firm and honest but gentle approach, beyond anything you may have experienced before.

The difference is called *family coupled with ministry*.

TWELVE

The Choir: Singing for Jesus and a Little Bit More!

PARENTS ARE NOT THE ONLY ONES WHO PLAY PSYCHOLOGIST. What child has not developed clever ways to manipulate mother so that she in turn convinces dad to be tolerant in regard to some situation? I did when I was a child and later was subjected to my children working their respective skills on Nikki and me. Family members can become real experts at furthering their own agendas within the framework of family. It's exactly the same in the Christian workplace.

We focus on the choir only to illustrate what happens when family members have a variety of motives or agendas in ministry. Similar illustrations could be gathered from any department of any ministry-type business or organization. If our goal is to rid the workplace of usury, it may be helpful to show how these personal ministry agendas can affect the lives of others.

When family members acquire an appetite for money or control, within the framework of ministry, personal agendas seem to surface. When one's livelihood is coupled with ministry, it is relatively easy to clutch at and seek to control one's turf, especially within family.

Today, the work of ministry may be extremely complex, even though it began in marvelous simplicity with the death and resurrection of Jesus Christ. It can become one's career, livelihood, financial investment, opportunity for power and control, financial security, social and spiritual fulfillment, and (I nearly forgot) response to the call of God.

Along the shores of the Sea of Galilee, Jesus saw Simon and his brother Andrew tending their fish nets. He said, "Follow Me, and I will make you fishermen for the souls of men." Scripture records that they left their work and followed Him. Your experience might have been similar. I took much longer than they did responding to His invitation, but the decision was the same. I said goodbye to financial security and benefits, a profession that I enjoyed, and a retirement plan that would have covered my needs.

In that initial "follow Me" decision, there is no thought of clutching after selfish agendas; one simply trusts Jesus or one doesn't. If you do you follow.

The promotion of personal agendas seems to occur after we have followed Jesus in ministry a while. Once we start to develop something of tangible value, we may find it difficult to hear His voice a second time saying, "Follow Me!" It's as though we say, "I left all to follow You once. How many times will I be asked to do this?"

When relationship problems develop within a pastor's family a tremendous career struggle occurs. Will he or she step down from the pulpit for a season, to spend time with the family? Some will. Even though their hearts pull them towards family, the temptation to clutch the security of position is often too great. Similarly, many times people remain in a ministry far too long, because they are afraid of the future. Too many cannot let go a second time—to follow Jesus! In the business world the struggle can be similar. For example, an employee may work hard and achieve the level of career position he or she desired, only to later experience relational problems of a "sibling" nature. In prayer they hear God say, "Follow Me." Leaving all to follow His leading is seldom easy.

An observation of ministry attitudes would almost cause us to conclude that Calvary's love was for the purpose of creating a few career tracks. Jesus made no specific financial or career guarantees to Simon and Andrew. Now as then, He merely asks us to live in such a way that we retain no agendas or attachments that would hinder us from following Him.

Today, the ministry can become one's career, livelihood, an opportunity for power and control, financial security, and social and spiritual fulfillment.

We have been commissioned by Jesus to "go into all the world and preach the gospel." No one is excluded from His invitation. We are challenged to be salt of the earth and light to the world. Each of us is compelled to minister God's love and grace to others. As part of this commitment, thousands of Christians volunteer for service in church ministries. Some become even more involved by making it their career. Jesus' message is the same to each of us, "Follow Me!" I'm not suggesting that God continuously asks members of His family to leave their jobs. I do suggest that He frequently asks us to leave self-centered agendas behind that hinder our effectiveness for Him.

You'll understand more fully what I mean as we now address the choir.

Life in a choir is a fulfilling experience for those who have no motive but to use their talents for God. However, it holds an expanded degree of both gratification and risk for those whose talent enables them to be featured as soloists.

I'll never forget my high school graduation. I played a trumpet solo with the accompaniment of a full orchestra, for the very first time. I practiced "The Lost Chord" until my lips ached. I practiced for weeks in anticipation of that special occasion. It was a thrilling experience for me and—to be honest, I enjoyed the applause and adulation from friends.

Choir members who are featured soloists have similar opportunities for service and personal gratification. As a result, their continued happiness is at greater risk than those not accustomed to the solo spot.

For example, when someone new joins the choir, everyone gives him or her a welcoming hug. But later, when they hear the new member sing in clear and melodious tones, a few of the hugs cease—probably someone's soloist turf has been threatened.

"This person is bound to get most of the solo spots from now on. You watch, the director will forget I'm even here!"

Somebody's turf has been threatened! This occurs when a person, "Sings for Jesus … and a little bit more!"

Those who sing for all the right reasons, and *only* the right reasons, will never feel threatened by another set of golden pipes.

Turf adjustments occur at every level of ministry, every day, wherever family members interact. Those who seldom enjoy the spotlight, or those who refuse to cling to the spotlight, will continue to welcome the newest member. Motives are extremely important. No doubt, that's one of the reasons Jesus taught us to position ourselves at the lower end of the banquet table: once we begin to claim seats of honor, we have created something to clutch.

I have a close pastor friend whose large church enjoys national visibility. A time came when, as senior pastor, he sensed some stress in his staff. Rather than harbor suspicions, he determined to discover why he felt he was being used by those closest to him. His unassuming and transparent style of leadership had helped him develop a close relationship with his staff. To his amazement, he discovered that some of his senior workers had a few personal ministry agendas that were not being satisfied. He learned that the reason they had encouraged him to take speaking engagements outside the city was not proof that

God was raising him to a national phase of ministry. Rather, he discovered those on his staff merely craved the opportunity to fill the pulpit at home. There was a slight problem. The senior pastor occupied the Sunday pulpit. Members of his staff wanted more than he could give. Relationships were at risk in this wonderful ministry, and all because of some unfulfilled personal agendas.

His solution was to expand the ministry. He designed a program to develop several sister churches throughout the country. Then he appointed some of these qualified brethren as senior pastors of each church. This was a tremendous solution! His unselfish, Nehemiah-like attitude enabled him to eliminate usury from his workplace and provide greater fulfillment for others in the process. He was able to deal effectively with the problem of usury because he was not a user of people.

Turf Protection

To me, it's always exciting to observe family members who celebrate their uniqueness, and happily radiate the love of God, while filling roles appropriate to their talents. People in ministry who know their calling enjoy an awesome degree of freedom and happiness. These people seldom feel the need to demand turf rights, because they know whatever they release to God will be restored in multiple blessings.

I've also seen God's children used, abused, and manipulated when others feel insecure in their ministry roles. I have seen family members lured into ministries, only to be dropped suddenly, all because of this same insecurity. Family members can become extremely jealous at times. There is a degree of competitiveness, and sometimes vindictiveness, that can occur between family members that often exceeds what is witnessed in the general marketplace. Is it that some family members have too much to hold on to? Or, is it that some have forgotten what to hold on to, where ministry is involved?

The Sermon on the Mount contains enough relational principles for us to follow that usury should not be an issue. However, we have a way of complicating many things Jesus intended to be simple. The blending of ministry, lifestyle, and financial success always creates relational challenges when Christians become unbalanced in their priorities.

Is it that some family members have too much to hold on to, or have forgotten what to hold on to where ministry is involved?

Jesus explained that family interacting with each other in love was to be the identity or marketing position for the family of God. Today we do research and marketing studies to help discover new and better ways to position Christianity to the world, even though Jesus has already provided us with the marketing concept acceptable to Him. His plan is—that we love one another! However, there is no reason to be discouraged, because the Gospel of Jesus Christ continues to be the only hope for the ills of this world. The fact that sibling rivalry rears its ugly head occasionally is no reflection on the authenticity of the Gospel. Christianity is real and life- changing! Relational risks occur primarily due to the understandable dynamics that occur when family works with family on a continuing basis. The job we are doing is still unequaled to any other in importance. My concern is that I see too many workers becoming weary from the relational stress of ministry. It's not the work that creates the fatigue—it's the presence of usury!

Whenever our motives in ministry exceed the intent of Jesus' invitation to us to minister usury will be present!

We, as family members, do not hold the copyright on Calvary or the Resurrection. The byproducts of Calvary should never be considered as ours to hoard. He holds the copyright! I see it this way.

As members of His family, our responsibilities require interaction with other family members. Each day brings the need for decisions, and each decision affects other family members. Our decisions usually process the thought, "How will this affect me?"

As we mentioned earlier, this is a logical question, because the work of ministry has developed into personal fulfillment, careers, livelihood, security, investment opportunities, retirement, power, control, visibility, and marketing opportunities. My point is that, because of the complications of material gain, it's nearly impossible for workers in ministry to make objective decisions about the future of their ministries.

I liken this to the decisions we make when driving a car. As long as our car is in a forward motion, all of our driving decisions are influenced by our direction of travel. To make objective decisions as to the wisest route to take, we sometimes should pull off to the curb, place the shift in neutral, take out our map, and study our options. From this neutral position we can make objective decisions. Have we gone too far? Could we do better using a different route? Should we turn around? Which exit will be the best?

Decisions that affect another member of God's family are extremely important to Him. Try as He does to speak to us, and provide us with objective input, we often don't hear because we are tuned only to that which will expedite us in the direction we are already going—that is, *our agenda.*

Abram's Turf Was Challenged

There was a time in Abram's life when he had a similar challenge. He had much at stake. Fortunately, he brought his mind and heart into neutral concerning his relational problem with Lot. He heard God's promise to him. As he weighed his options, he felt God speaking to his heart telling him not to clutch, but to let Lot have the good pastureland surrounding Jordan's banks. He then decided to move his family into a land with which he was not familiar. He didn't have to do this. He had a choice. Any number of today's financial consultants would have told Abram to protect his turf, to state his position legally if necessary. Had Abram obeyed this type of counsel, he would have missed all that God had planned for him. Instead, he brought himself into a neutral position before God, and heard God whisper to his heart.

Trapped by the complexities of material gain, It's nearly impossible for those in ministry to make objective decisions regarding God's will for their ministries.

A few years ago, my wife and I were enjoying lunch at a restaurant and couldn't help overhearing the conversation in the adjacent booth. A middle-aged daughter had taken her father—who was hard of hearing—out for lunch. The daughter was forced to speak loudly to her father. "Dad, when are you going to buy a hearing aid? You're really becoming quite deaf!"

The father quickly and loudly responded, "Daughter, I like it just the way it is! I see you and your brother fighting all the time and I just don't want to hear any of it! I'm totally happy the way things are!"

I think that story adequately describes a few of our situations. Many times we are guilty of ministering for Jesus (and a little bit more), and we really don't want to hear what God may have to say about some of our decisions. So we keep driving as fast as we can, in the direction we want to go.

Once putting my mind in neutral and listening possibly saved my life.

My wife and I owned a radio station in a city on the coast

of British Columbia. Our radio station's transmitter was located on an island about five miles from the mainland. It provided excellent coverage, but was difficult to service. One morning when the transmitter developed problems, I called our engineer and arranged for a trip to the transmitter site. To our dismay, because of an intensely heavy fog that had settled in, the ferry to the island had been cancelled. Our only option was to take the engineer's small, twelve-foot outboard and hope for the best.

We calculated the north-south movement of the tide and, with the help of a small compass, started out.

Have you ever completely lost your sense of direction? Well, I did that day. We traveled about four or five miles toward the island but, the farther we proceeded, the denser the fog became. I felt totally helpless. We were entirely socked in—the visibility was only about six feet. The fog horns wailed their mournful sound: ocean liners and tug boats slowly plied their way north or south along that inside channel. They relied solely on radar to keep them on course.

Our transmitter was located on the northern tip of the island. To pass that tip would send us west into the main ocean channel of the Malispina Strait, a body of water about twenty miles across. (The ocean liners that travel between Vancouver and Alaska use this particular channel. They would have no way of seeing us, or even knowing our whereabouts, if we drifted into their path.) It would be untruthful to say I wasn't scared.

My engineer knew the approximate speed of his small boat. When, by his calculations, he figured we had traveled about five miles, he cut his motor.

With concern in his voice, he said, "Don, I think we're close now, but with this fog there is no way of knowing, *so we have nothing left to do but listen!* If we're close to shore at all, we should be able to hear the waves splashing on the shore. If we've drifted too far north, we could land on the wrong island. If we can't find land to the north or south, we could be in real trouble!"

The ocean was utterly calm. I could see my friend and he

could see me, but, beyond that, we could see nothing else but fog. Our only hope for survival was to identify land by the sound of small waves gently splashing on the shoreline. We listened. No we listened *hard!* The next sound we heard might be that of an approaching ocean liner or it might be the splashing sounds from the island.

I don't know how long we sat in silence, not making a sound, just listening. Perhaps it was about a half hour later that, to my left and his right, we both heard a gentle sound like water lapping against a shore. We listened until we were certain of the sound and its direction. We started the engine and slowly moved in that direction. In a few minutes we had identified the rocky shoreline of our island. We had found our bearings—we were safe!

Listening hard that day saved our lives. Listening hard today could save your ministry!

Would you set this book aside for a few moments and see if you can place your mind in neutral? It's not an easy thing I'm asking—perhaps because we do it so rarely. When we take a vacation, it usually requires the first week just to reach a place where we quit thinking about our work or ministry. Reaching a true neutral is not easy—but is worth doing.

When you're ready, consider this:

The action taken by Nehemiah established the principle that—even at the risk of making decisions that do not provide maximum financial benefit, or help us achieve our personal or ministry goals—relationships between members of God's family must be protected and maintained.

If you listen closely and set all self-serving agendas aside—just like that day in the fog, when we heard the gentle splashings of the ocean on that shoreline—you'll be able to hear the gentle voice of God saying, "This is the way . . . follow Me!" The listening process is extremely important because, to the extent that our decisions reflect our Father's will, we gain an understanding of His love.

Jesus had no agenda but us when He considered Calvary.

THIRTEEN

The Spotlight is On Us!

EVERY PASTOR KNOWS IT'S NO FUN RAISING A FAMILY UNDER the watchful eyes of the congregation. In fact, the moment parents are known to be Christians, they become the focus of their neighbors and friends. Meeting the Christian expectations of those we know is difficult—and may seem a little unfair. People active in the Christian workplace are also in the spotlight. The spotlight of the world is focused on members of God's family. He planned it this way.

In America, it is almost commonplace for stadiums or convention centers to be filled with people worshipping God at some Christian event. Participants travel great distances to attend. The air is charged with excitement about what God is doing, and what He's about to do. The music starts and, as with one voice, thousands join together in worship. Hearts melt in the atmosphere of praise.

Soon life on the outside is forgotten as each becomes immersed in the impact of this inspiring event.

To the casual observer, everyone's voice seems to blend in song with the thousands who surround them, but God notices something wrong. He discerns some that would find it very awkward worshipping side by side with other family members in that very same stadium. Their relationships have been marred through interaction with other Christians they have worked with in ministry. They have been on one side or the other of usury and have not been willing or able to fix the damage. They are able to worship with those they have never met before, but not with those who know them best. These individuals can make powerful statements for Christianity, if they are willing.

Crowds seldom convince. Individuals accomplishing the unusual do!

No wonder Jesus said the identity tag for members of His Family would be brethren interacting with each other in love. People notice this! In the following chapter I make mention of a lady who asked how Nikki and I have enjoyed marriage together for over thirty-five years. This was important to her because she knew it didn't "just happen." In fact, my wife paid a price of love, patience, understanding and forgiveness—more than some are willing to pay. When we visit with Christian friends at the end of a church service, it's easy to say, "Hi, Harry, how's it going!" But if you work with Harry, day after day, and if you and Harry recently applied for the same position, which Harry won, it's a little harder to give him that same, sincere, friendly salutation. It costs more, but is noticed.

If the world is to be turned onto Christ, the marketing billboards must tell a story that will connect with people. Jesus implied that these "billboards" would feature His brethren, sometimes competing, but always remaining friends. In other words—interacting in love.

So here it is—the challenge of a lifetime!

You were probably first introduced to the Gospel by Christians in the normal routine of life. The Christian workplace provides such an opportunity. This is not a stage production, nor does it feature skilled orators or musicians. It's a real-life performance.

Whether one is a volunteer in a local church or a staff member of a Christian company, each competitive encounter with siblings is a scene that one enjoys more than the other. The Christian who owns an auto repair shop, and employs a few Christian mechanics, is where identity statements are made for God's family. The customers know that honesty, integrity, and friendliness, are qualities that reflect character and respect. This is worth noticing. Identity statements are made for Christ when ministries or Christian-type companies compete—when one gains and another loses, but friendships continue. These workplace relationships are worth noticing for they cost something. Crowds seldom convince. Individuals accomplishing the unusual do! We have four challenges before us:

- ◆ To fulfill our workplace responsibilities;
- ◆ To represent Christ, professionally and otherwise;
- ◆ To eliminate usury from the workplace;
- ◆ To create an environment of healing for those who have previously suffered injury through usury.

We have been assigned a responsibility that far exceeds our particular workplace tasks. Ours is the opportunity to exhibit to the world the Family of God relating with each other in the manner God intended.

This is a statement the world will notice!

Many Christian workplaces have employees who do not profess Christianity. Each ministry has workers in various stages of Christian commitment and maturity. None can receive a more compelling message as to the validity of Christianity than to observe members of God's family resisting usury and relating to one another with love and respect. Show us the Christian workplace where no one places unrealistic obligations on another, and where self-serving agendas are set aside, and we'll observe a segment of family that is making a tremendous impact for Christ.

We are exposed to many religions, causes and persuasions. How does one decide which is right? What will guide me toward Jesus? A workplace free from usury will provide very persuasive evidence of the authenticity of Jesus Christ.

I did not realize when I accepted a position in the Christian workplace that I accepted a world evangelism assignment. But, I believe I did. Someone said to me recently, "Cartmell, I can see your footprints all over the place." That's true for each of us. It's true enough that it's sometimes frightening. Whenever we mingle with people, we leave footprints of influence. If we are known to be Christians, whatever footprints we leave will be perceived by some as Christian identity. It is little wonder that, with the complexity of Christian lifestyles that exist in a materialistic, control-driven society, we seldom see a genuine spiritual revival.

When we are known to be Christians, whatever footprints we leave will be perceived by some as Christian identity.

No one has a better opportunity to correct some of the misconceptions about Jesus than those involved in His family business.

Say you've accepted a position as a Sunday school teacher. Your role is of worldwide dimension, because of the ripple affect your life has, as those in your class move to other parts of the world—first impacted by the Christ in you! You have a business. Your role is greater than that of your primary product or service. You and your team have the opportunity to establish the true identity of God's family for many confused customers.

When God drew us into His workplace, He had designs that went beyond the actual work or ministry at hand. He commissioned each of us with an important role in marketing His grace and forgiveness. Calvary was a local scene that took place just outside Jerusalem, but its impact continues to affect millions of people. Your workplace may also be local but has the potential of expanding your ministry's reach to worldwide proportions. Be encouraged!

FOURTEEN

We Can Do It!

THERE ARE TIMES IN EVERY FAMILY WHEN RELATIONSHIPS become broken or strained. Christian families do their best to mend these broken fences and bring healing to these relationships. They're usually quite successful because the love of God enables them to forgive. Forgiven people can do this. They can be extremely effective repairing and strengthening family relationships, whether at home or in the workplace.

I recall getting my hair cut by a lady who has known my wife and me for several years. During the cutting session she paused and asked me, "Don, how many years have you and Nikki been married?"

I responded, "Thirty-five."

The room became silent. Others had heard my response. A young lady working in another section of the shop said, "I don't know you, but can you tell me the secret of making a marriage work that long?"

I thought for a moment and replied, "Respect."

Again there was silence, which I eventually broke by adding, "I believe a couple should cling to each other loosely enough that neither feels taken for granted."

I didn't think there was anything very profound in my

remarks but it became the subject of conversation of those in the shop for the rest of the day.

In this final chapter I want to focus on your relationships with the Christians you associate with in work or ministry. We have concluded that family relationships are sometimes delicate—but always worth preserving. I hope we agreed that ridding a workplace of usury provides an atmosphere conducive to the building of healthy associations. Finally, I suggest that *respect* is the foundation of this entire process.

Respect: The Key to Workplace Relationships

Each radio station where I have worked had one thing in common: dissension among departments. I found that few workers ever took the time to understand the other person's role. They had little respect for those in the other departments.

At one point in my broadcasting career, we served a relatively small market. For the size of the market we had a fabulous staff. Our morning man/program director Jim, was a university graduate with a degree in broadcast communications. He was very good. Our sales staff was not large, but we had a few people who really knew how to sell. One account executive Harry, had an unusual talent for sales. As a result, he began making fairly good money. Resentment and jealousy developed. The program director eventually concluded that he had discovered some inequities in the workplace—namely, that the sales department was the place to be if you wanted to make good money.

One day Jim came to my office and requested a transfer to sales. He said, "I know that if Harry can do it, with my experience and education, I should be able to do it better than he can. Please give me a chance to sell."

I did. I gave him some good accounts as starters to encourage him in his new selling role. We covered his air shift—Jim was on his way!

About two weeks later Jim returned to my office. He was

upset. His voice was nervous and trembling. He said, "Don, can I please have my old job back? I can't handle it on the streets. I have worked hard preparing good sales presentations, but wherever I go, store managers refuse to buy from me. I can't handle the rejection!" He added, "Evidently Harry can do it and people buy from him, but they won't buy from me!"

I gave him his old job back. He never complained again. In just two weeks he acquired a respect for Harry and, also, for himself. I noticed that he began to focus proudly on the uniqueness of his own talents and abilities. He finally realized that success for him would come by maximizing the talents he possessed, so he ceased comparing himself with Harry. Respect made the difference. They continued as friends. A wonderful relationship was placed at risk, because Jim didn't understand and respect the talents and abilities of Harry.

Years ago, while employed as a personnel officer, I conducted a survey of four hundred workers. Of those, 80 percent indicated they did not enjoy their jobs and felt it was too late for them to learn another trade. They were frustrated, feeling imprisoned by circumstances. Imagine, over three hundred of those employees went to work each day wishing they could do the job that someone else was doing.

I have often wondered how many were just like Jim, craving opportunities for which they were not suited. In the Christian workplace it is even more important that workers find satisfaction and fulfillment. The apostle Paul admonishes us to honestly assess and acknowledge our gifts. The distribution of gifts was not by accident. God has a plan for every life and has distributed gifts to each, according to His purposes.

The mass media—magazines, radio and television—tend to highlight the careers of successful leaders. It is easy to conclude from this that real success is to be found only in significant leadership or management roles. Forgotten is the reality that, for every successful leader, dozens of gifted individuals are needed to perform tasks for which the leader is not suited.

Respect Is Needed in a Variety of Ways

Proper respect among Christians involves an almost inexhaustible number of variables,

1. The basic respect due everyone. No one should be used, abused or taken for granted.
2. Respect is due for special achievements, talents, and accomplishments. Many find it difficult to respect people they don't like. If one deserves some recognition for an outstanding accomplishment, we should give it to them.
3. Respect for those who have a distinct relationship to us. This means our pastors, employers, supervisors, professors, parents, civic leaders, and so on.
4. Respect for those who worship with us, who come to our home groups or Sunday school classes. These are people who have at least some spiritual goals or values similar to our own.

Together, we could list additional areas where respect is needed, such as:

1. Respect for another person's time.
2. Respect for a person's need for privacy.
3. Respect for the right of others to have opinions different from our own.

Let's mention one more: respect the right of others to succeed in all that they do, and possibly surpass us in our own field of expertise!

I believe it was back in the 60's that Paul Harvey made a long-play recording on the subject of democracy. In it he stated something to the effect that, in communism all men are equal but in a democracy all men are created equal but have the opportunity to become unequal!

Ideally, Christians will be encouraged to run a good race to win, not with the motive of winning over another, but simply to win. Each person should aspire to reach both personal and corporate goals.

Relational Success Can Be Yours—with God's Help!

As with any family situation, life has no guarantees. Occasionally our plans go awry despite our best efforts. As Christians, we have the tremendous advantage of knowing that the love and wisdom of God are available to guide and direct our paths. His help is as good as it comes!

- He provides strength and grace to help bring healing and protection to ministry or workplace relationships.
- He gives grace to forgive and forget.

When I was about twelve, my Cocker spaniel and I were great companions. We had a special relationship, and went everywhere together. One day we hiked up into the woods behind our home. My dog caught the scent of some animal and went after it. It turned out to be a raccoon, and my dog got the worst of it. She returned with her face torn and bleeding. As my dog's best friend, I went to comfort her, but, to my surprise, she growled angrily at me and would have bitten me had I moved closer. Something was wrong here. She had never done this before. I wasn't the one who tore up her face—surely she knew that! Why couldn't I get close? I remember well the feeling of rejection I experienced that day.

Finally, the dog, trembling with pain, lay down about 8 feet from me under a large alder tree. She wasn't happy, nor was I. Broken-hearted, I moved as close as I could without causing her to growl and show her teeth. I thought to myself, "I don't understand what's going on here, but I'll wait you out, because you're my friend." Before long I fell asleep under that same tree, not far from my estranged dog.

I was awakened by the sensation of warm breath on my hand. I looked and saw my dog slowly inching her way toward me. I just waited and in a few minutes she was licking my hand. From that point we were OK. Our friendship resumed.

I still remember that scene, because on that occasion I knew I was doing everything I could to restore that friendship. I stretched out my hand and waited. I was there for my dog and made it as easy as possible to fix things between us.

Sometimes, when family members get injured, they lash out at everyone—even their closest friends. It takes a special kind of love and patience to promote healing in those situations. Sometimes the most helpful action we can take is to be still, be available—and wait, just as God does.

- ◆ He gives wisdom, if He knows we'll be receptive to His ideas.
- ◆ He gives us His peace.

I visited one of our radio stations where the staff was in a turmoil over some recent changes. I flew into town, and asked the general manager to call a staff meeting. As the staff members filed into the conference room, I saw their expressions. Some were sullen, some frustrated, and others wore cynical expressions, as if to say, "Let's get this over with!" The majority of those attending the meeting were Christians. This was family!

In a few minutes I joined them, and—as it happened, we had an excellent meeting. Problems were solved and most attitudes seemed to change. After the meeting a member of the staff said to me, "Mr. Cartmell, I don't understand it, but when you entered the conference room today, the room became peaceful."

I understood. I draw on this gift from Jesus often. Just before His ascension He said, "My peace I leave with you." His peace is available to us today. What a difference it can make in our workplace relationships.

He gives special insights to help us resolve workplace conflicts that may occur. He cares! After all, we're a part of His family!

Evidently the Jews in Nehemiah's day had become weary with all the pressures of life. They had lost the spark, enthusiasm, and pride in their spiritual heritage as family. They were just living life. Many felt trapped by circumstances. Some were becoming wealthy at the expense of their brethren, but for many life wasn't fun anymore. Most had forgotten the significance of who they were in God. They had lost their identity as individuals. This was more tragic than a city without walls.

God gave Nehemiah special insight into the core problems. He knew just what to do.

The wall needed to be rebuilt, but first, the people needed a fresh sense of their own identity. The elimination of usury brought this about. They were made to realize that the only reason the usury was stopped was because they were members of God's family. Members of God's family are just as significant today, in the eyes of God. His intentions for His family continue!

The blending of ministry with ego, power, money, and control continues to cause relational stress. Some of us have gone through many tough battles, and we're a little weary and on edge. Life hasn't always been easy. Recently I talked with a friend who had just visited his doctor because of deep chest pains. The diagnosis was stress! Where did the stress originate? The Christian workplace! Even working in a church can lose its exciting edge. It can become just another stressful job of answering the telephone, filing papers, writing letters, visiting people in the hospital, officiating at weddings and funerals, and teaching. Studying the Bible for sermon preparation can become work. Singing in the choir can lose its edge. In the radio business it's just the same. What we do can become just a format. I don't know how many times I've interviewed applicants for positions in Christian radio, and asked, "Have you ever done this kind of radio before?"

The applicant replies, "No, but I'm a professional, and a format is a format. If you can do one, you can do them all!"

How I wished I could have explained that what we do is much more than just another format. The concept for the format itself was birthed at Calvary.

Usury must stop. Many of us need fresh reasons to become excited about our identity again. For various reasons, weeks may go by when nothing much happens at work to make us feel special. But we are family! God's family! We are as special to God as we should be to each other.

Some Things Should Be Sorted Out Personally

Working with other Christians, on various ministry projects, made me keenly aware of the care and attention required if workplace relationships were to be protected. I have participated in meetings that pitted Christians against Christians on matters involving ministry or business issues. Some didn't handle this well. Some did. I found it necessary to establish personal integrity boundaries that I would not cross, just to protect these valued relationships. I wrestled my way through some of these fine lines for the sake of family. You may want to do the same.

When Jesus prayed for His disciples, He asked that they "would not be taken from this world, but rather be kept in the world." I reasoned that the work I was doing was important, and that God intended for us to stay here and do His bidding. Therefore, there must be a way to do this and protect His family relationships at the same time.

The Workplace is Worldwide

In America we are probably exposed to usury of a financial nature more than in less affluent countries. However, taking advantage of those closest to us is a universal temptation—and another form of usury. Therefore, I reasoned, there must be a way to execute our responsibilities within the culture and society we are in. Our relationship with God and family starts right where we are.

I Will Be Affected by the Success of Others

I will be affected by the success of other Christians. Conversely, my decisions will also affect them. Family relationships will change as a result of family interaction. I will be misunderstood or misjudged by members of the Christian family. I also will be guilty of misjudging the actions of others. I must develop my own guidelines by which to protect family to the best of my ability.

I Must Fine-Tune My Priorities

Jesus did not die for the organization or company that I represent, regardless of its ministry value. He gave His life for ME! His family is made up of people, not organizations. My priorities should be similar. According to Nehemiah, family relationships come first.

I Will Anticipate Change

Leaders of Christian businesses and organizations strive for success. There will be growth—and change! This will affect me, sometimes good and sometimes not so good.

My Commitment

To the best of my ability, I will not impose usury on other members of God's family. If I detect myself becoming calloused toward those affected by anything my work calls me to do—I will leave that particular place of work or ministry, rather than become hardened or cynical. I will not return until I am ready to extend coworkers in ministry the love and respect appropriate to members of God's family.

Because of the importance of God's family, and the significance of the work I am called to do, this became my commitment. I suppose it entails seeing the big picture! How we relate to others really is important. A friend mentioned to me the importance of establishing boundaries in our lives, which become foundations for all major decisions. Accordingly, I recognized that "relating with members of God's family in love" should be a principle that would give definition to my life. God gave us some ground rules for how we are to relate with members of His family. It is up to us to make this happen.

Who bats a thousand? I certainly don't. Many are the hours I have spent with family members in an effort to preserve or restore workplace relationships. You've likely done the same.

I realize that this book is being read by a wide spectrum of Christians. Whatever your role in ministry, whether salaried or volunteer, full-time or part-time, leadership or support staff, I hope we agree on these important points:

1. Ours is a family situation.
2. Some form of usury develops whenever and wherever Christians work together on a continuing basis. It comes by being family.
3. Many times the demands or obligations placed on Christians exceed what is reasonable or just.
4. As a leader, you probably remember times when you manipulated members of your staff, and even used the power of ministry to leverage people in their decisions. I did.
5. You have witnessed the damage cause by secret agendas within ministry.
6. Because of the importance of "who we are," and the significance of the work we are doing in ministry, usury needs to go!

Are You Ready to Respond to Nehemiah's Call to Action?

A. The process start's at the top—with the leader.

Because Nehemiah was not guilty of exacting usury from those he supervised, he was able to say to the others, "Stop it!" and "Give it back!" He was able to hear the cries from his workers.

B. Those injured through usury sought help from a righteous leader. It is essential for workers to cry out on this issue. Just pray you have a Nehemiah as a leader.

C. All agreed to stop the usury, which is a tremendous credit to Nehemiah's style of leadership.

With usury properly dealt with, Nehemiah's wall building project was completed in record time. The elimination of usury brings fresh energy to any situation.

A Miracle in Human Relations!

Think for a moment of the financial adjustments made at Nehemiah's request, for two reasons:

To restore family relations and to confirm how significant they were in the eyes of God. (This hasn't changed.)

- ✦ Mortgages were torn up
- ✦ People returned homes, lands, and vineyards to their original owners. (property that had legally changed ownership).
- ✦ Sizeable amounts of interest were refunded.
- ✦ Financial arrangements on loans were revised eliminating the high interest rates.
- ✦ Those taken as slaves were returned to their homes.

In your church, organization, or business, ridding the workplace of usury will (we hope) not require adjustments of this magnitude.

If You Are in Leadership

- You will likely need to make a few upward adjustments to salaries to remove inequities.
- Retroactive pay adjustments may also be in order. Family members typically procrastinate on matters of this nature.
- Perhaps you should give some thought to retirement benefits for workers of long-term or vital service.
- What about bonuses for work well done? Do your workers know how much they are appreciated?
- You may have people in supervisory roles who are not qualified. Look into it.
- Your expectations of some workers may need to be adjusted downward so that you no longer assess their efforts through your "perfectionist" eyes. Most perfectionists do not necessarily have a better way of doing things—they just insist on having things done their way! (I got that attitude knocked out of me during my teenage years.)
- Beyond these suggestions, you may simply need to remove your leadership "blinders", so that you actually see and appreciate those in your team. Take time to tell them!
- You may find it necessary to lower the benefits of some workers in order to restore financial equity to the workplace. Nehemiah convinced his nobles that, within the family of God, some should not gain at the expense of others.
- It may be necessary for those on the ministry board to correct inequities in the pastor's income and benefits.

You can only imagine the enthusiasm these changes will infuse into your organization. Many personal agendas will fade away, as they will no longer be necessary. There is no need to clutch when you feel safe.

Your challenge is nothing compared to that which Nehemiah faced. Believe me, it is win-win all the way!

If You Are Part of the Volunteer or Paid Support Staff

You may be saying, "I'm not in a leadership role. This doesn't apply to me." Wrong! In a very real sense, each of us is in leadership. We influence people every day. We solicit their trust, so that others will follow our lead. We have a dual role to perform when it comes to the matter of usury.

- First, stop being used or manipulated. We each have our own *box of tools* and can decide where and how to use them. You may need to call out to your Nehemiah, or be prepared to confront when necessary.
- Remember, if you don't have a Nehemiah for a leader, things may not get resolved and you may have to leave. If you don't have a Nehemiah, workplace relations will continue to deteriorate. It's a hard decision, unique to a family business.
- Ensure that you don't use or manipulate your leaders or coworkers, by expecting from them that which is unreasonable.
- Be prepared to reduce your expectations of the people you work with, so you don't require them to live up to unrealistic standards.
- Eliminate your own secret agendas. They only set you up for disappointment.

A Call to Everyone to Participate

Everyone should cooperate in this project, because, after all, it is our family!

We have never witnessed the explosive impact a ministry can make for God's kingdom when the entire membership of a church or Christian workplace is in accord. About the closest thing I have witnessed to a group of people being in accord was in the lobby of the Torrance Hospital some fifteen years ago. My wife had been admitted. The Xrays and MRIs indicated the need for major surgery. We obtained the finest surgeon available.

A few days prior to the scheduled surgery, some of the ladies from the church I pastored asked if they could come to the hospital and pray in the lobby during surgery. Naturally, I said, "Please come!"

I'll never forget the scene. I walked with my wife to the OR door and, with a heavy heart, returned to the waiting area. In the far corner of the room I saw a group of several ladies with their heads bowed. There were no agendas—just a reaching out to God on behalf of my wife.

Sometime later the surgeon appeared, looking frustrated and angry.

He said, "Mr. Cartmell, I specialize in this type of surgery. I teach it at the UCLA Medical Center. I reviewed all the charts and knew what I was going after. But when I performed the surgery all I could find were two small pieces of withered tissue. There was nothing there, but I know what the results of the MRI and other tests were! This is naturally good news for you and your wife, but it annoys me, as a doctor, that I didn't find what I knew was there."

I looked over to the far end of the hospital lobby, where these women continued in prayer. I shook the doctor's hand and made my way over to share the good news with my friends.

Only God knows the impact our efforts might have for the Kingdom of God, if our ministry workplaces could be rid of usury and self-serving agendas. It can, and should, start with us! Our relationships with family can become everything Jesus predicted: people relating with each other in love.

Tomorrow, when you return to your job, may you view your fellow workers with added significance. See people, but even more than that, see members of a very special family!

You may work with people who tax your patience beyond

what is reasonable, but if they are family, they are immeasurably important to God—and should be to us.

Organizational and business decisions must be made, but I hear God saying to us through His promises, that it is possible to do the work of ministry, and meet all of His expectations without imposing usury on family members.

When Usury is Removed Workplace Efficiency Will Improve Dramatically

Once Nehemiah dealt with the usury problem, a synergism resulted that brought the wall-building project to completion in miracle time! *"Our enemies lost their self-confidence, because they realized that this work had been done with the help of our God." (Nehemiah 6:16)*

We'll enjoy similar results. We will discover that we can address the bottom line, scrutinize the growth of our churches and organizations, make all the decisions necessary in a successful ministry, publishing company or relief organization, without expecting more from each other that what is reasonable.

Starting with You and Me, Usury Can Be Reduced

If we eliminate at least some of the workplace stress caused by usury—and we can—we have the satisfaction of knowing that our efforts have been in sync with the very heart of God.

Do we need a greater reason?

FIFTEEN

Relationship Success Keys

Relationship Success Key No.1

For me, the acknowledgment of the family dynamic in the Christian workplace made it easier to discover the pathway to success. This awareness enabled me to process relational challenges through the filter of family.

Understanding the uniqueness of your workplace enables you to exercise good judgement in relational matters. When relational challenges occur, think family! Within the family dynamic you'll discover both the reason and the solution.

Relationship Success Key No. 2

Customs and technology change from one generation to the next, but relational matters within families continue about the same. Those who worked with Nehemiah reached the place where they were willing to confront him because of the usury situation. Loving confrontation is essential when rebuilding or maintaining family relationships.

Therefore learn the art of "loving confrontation." As soon as problems are identifiable, they should be addressed.

Relational Success Key No. 3

Relational success for workers in ministry requires us to acknowledge that we are each found somewhere between what we know to do—and what we do, as Christians. We are influenced by family, peers, friends, and circumstances. We are in transition. Be willing to adjust your expectations of others so that you are able to acknowledge their progress.

Relational Success Key No.4

Whether in leadership, a supervisory role, or some other workplace capacity, commit to radiating the unchanging love of God. This isn't just spiritual talk—it is practical workplace advice. Lives in transition need an anchor to relate to. People in the Christian workplace encounter spiritual warfare on the "outside" and on the "inside." It's easy to become a bit edgy and lose one's bearings. Workers need a supervisor or co-worker to help them keep an even keel. This is done by example. Workers, whose lives serve as attitude adjusters for others enjoy relational success.

Relational Success Key No. 5

Success for leaders requires an understanding of their own unique characteristics, their focus, energy and drive. This understanding should make them alert to their dependency on others. They should also remember that both their strengths and weaknesses create stress in the workplace.

Success for workers equally requires an understanding of these same characteristics of their leaders. This way, they will be inclined to adjust their relational expectations so that much of what they could perceive to be usury will be identified only as the consequence of growth.

Relational Success Key No. 6

Success in an entrepreneurial work environment requires that you understand who your leader is, and know who you are, so that you can take ownership of your decisions. Otherwise, you will end up feeling used.

Try to accept your workplace environment as it is and discover how to function happily within it. Then season it with Christian love.

It is a mistake to emulate your leader in ways that are not natural to who you are. Be yourself, and be proud of your own uniqueness! Expand in skills and knowledge, and recognize that your unique abilities came from God. Develop relationships upon this foundation.

Relational Success Key No. 7

Learn to identify your true enemies. Unless you are continuously alert to the fact that, in your ministry workplace, you are interfacing with members of God's family, you are certain to make some wrong judgment calls.

A few months ago I put my quarter into an arcade game where I held the gun in my hand and, at a moment's notice, had to decide to shoot or not shoot, dependent upon whether I thought I was looking at a good guy or a bad guy.

I shot a few good guys. It gave me a sick feeling. We do this a lot in the Christian workplace.

Family members with selfish agendas may at times be enemies of the workplace, but we really need to be sure. Ask God to help you discern between the real enemy, (Satan) and some imperfect Christians. Ask Him to give you the patience and discipline not to get trigger-happy.

Relational success Key No. 8

Lower your expectations of family members until you can be impressed by their achievements.

Because of the closeness of family relationships, we tend to take each other for granted. Relationships improve when our expectations of others are brought to a realistic level. By allowing some added space for the imperfections of others, we'll discover that they'll do the same for us.

Relational Success Key No. 9

Enjoy the freedom to ask yourself financial type questions without feeling guilty, even though your work involves ministry.

I like to think that success in ministry will enable you to

reflect back on your many years of service with no regrets.

Most people receive far less financial remuneration in the Christian workplace than their counterparts in the general market. If earnings are not sufficient to meet family needs, why continue working there, unless you know you are exactly where God wants you to be? If you do—you're in great shape!

Relational Success Key No. 10

Be aware of the potential for sibling rivalry. It is a normal occurrence within families. It is a family enterprise!

Learn to love and relate as family, but work together as though you were next-door neighbors. You know each other very well, but not well enough to take each other for granted.

Relational Key No. 11

Whether a leader, manager, or supervisor, qualify yourself for the role you are filling. Family members find it difficult to take direction from siblings they consider incompetent.

Relational Success Key No. 12

Regardless of whether you are in a volunteer ministry or a part of paid staff, try to interview your potential leaders or supervisors until you are satisfied they can lead you higher up the ladder of success in ministry.

The more comfortable you are accepting their leadership, the better. Family relations are wonderful but somewhat delicate. So remember, the fact that your work involves ministry does not eliminate the family dynamic from the workplace. Relational risks are a reality.

Relational Success Key No. 13

As a leader, be honest, sensitive, caring, and fair, but above all be timely in the supervision of family. In the Christian workplace the tendency too often is to procrastinate when it comes to addressing relational problems. Deal with relational situations when they are small and correctable. Delay—and you may be too late. You're dealing with family! Ephesians 4:26 says, "let not the sun go down upon your wrath." Be punctual!

Relational Success Key No. 14

Learn to reflect the happiness of God, because in the workplace, good things happen to happy people.

Everyone enjoys working with happy people. Happiness is contagious and is a tremendous stepping stone to success. People love to follow happy people!

Relational Success Key No. 15

He who has the best attitude wins!

One cannot successfully address usury in the workplace without first adopting a positive and healthy attitude towards others.

Good family relationships are built on a positive attitude!

Success Key No. 16

Submit your personal agendas to God. Don't impose them on others in the workplace.

We who have felt led into some form of ministry work occasionally have a few secret aspirations we want to accomplish for God—or ourselves. It may seem feasible to use the workplace to fulfill a few of these. Lasting success in the Christian workplace comes to those who do not clutch to those things for which they do not hold the copyright. **Jesus holds the copyright to Calvary!**

Relational Success Key No. 17

The importance of who we are as members of God's family and the significance of what we are doing in ministry, will always provide "reason" to relate to one another in love. Therefore soberly consider what type of "footprints" you leave in your daily travels.

I was speaking with someone recently about the tremendous testimony made by the Billy Graham team. In my early teens I kept an autograph book. Leafing through it recently, I noticed Dr. Graham's signature. Below it he had written Psalm 16:11. This was 1947. He was just starting out as an evangelist. For over fifty years this team has left "footprints" around the world that reflect their commitment of love to God and each other. What footprints!

My mother left similar "footprints." Hers were not left in the great coliseums of the world, but rather in the beer parlors of British Columbia, where, each Saturday night, in her Salvation Army uniform, she witnessed Christ to the needy in Vancouver. Her "footprints" were also left in rural one-room schoolhouses, where she and my father conducted Sunday schools. Her life was a commitment to family and ministry.What beautiful footprints!

Mine—others will have to assess them when I'm gone. But I do have today, and what a marvelous opportunity is mine to reflect the true identity of God's family.

Relational Success Key No. 18

Learn to respect everyone in your workplace, whether or not you particularly like him or her. Try to think as highly about other members of God's family as He does.

We seldom "use" people that we respect.

Relational Success Key No. 19

Surround yourself with successful, positive people, hopefully from outside your particular workplace. Give them license to counsel, pray with you, and guide you in your Christian walk.

You can't be your most effective without the support of others. Nobody can!

Relational Key No. 20

Invest some "prime time" in worship and devotion to Jesus every day. It's His workplace. We're members of His family.

No one desires loving and caring family relationships more than He does.

He will give you wisdom and grace sufficient for each day.